Colin Mudie Power Boats

Colin Mudie
Power Boats

Hamlyn
London New York Sydney Toronto

Published by
The Hamlyn Publishing Group Limited
London · New York · Sydney · Toronto
Astronaut House, Feltham, Middlesex, England
© Copyright The Hamlyn Publishing Group Limited, 1975

ISBN 0 600 37045 3

Type set in England by Filmtype Services Limited, Scarborough

Printed in Czechoslovakia

Contents

The Development of Speed Boats 6   *Power for Luxury Craft 20*
Modern Power Boat Racing 60   *Modern Yachts 81*

front endpapers: The American excursion paddle steamer *Grand Republic*. The people on board are watching the America's Cup Race of 1895.
back endpapers: The 1972 power boat marathon race at Southampton.
half-title page: An MTU 8V diesel in its marine form and fitted with a ZF reduction gearbox which delivers over 80 h p.
title page: Unowot, winner of the 1973 Cowes/Torquay/Cowes race.
contents page. The 1966 Daily Express Offshore Power Boat Race winner *Ghostrider*. The hand belongs to Bob Sherbert, the engineer, whose ankles were broken as the boat bounced through rough seas.

Yacht Design Round the World 30   *Engines and Installations* 40
Index and Acknowledgments 96

The Development of Speed Boats

The remarkable *Miss England* which with a single 930-hp Napier Lion engine had a speed of over 90 mph.

It is difficult for us, after three generations of power boating, to realise how slowly our ancestors had to make their way about the sea. Five, six, seven and eight knots were once normal maximums and twelve knots from a racing skiff and eighteen knots from a large full rigged clipper ship counted as record breaking. Of course, even ashore natural high speeds were quite modest, with a man running up to 20 mph and a horse running up to thirty, but generally life ashore and afloat proceeded along at speeds not far away from man's walking pace. At sea the natural difficulties of adverse winds and contrary currents made seafaring at such low speeds often a matter of tactical as much as practical skills.

The earliest engines, because of their general inefficiency, were extremely large and cumbersome for their output and also unsuitable for use afloat in terms of safety. Wooden craft, heavily tarred, lived in great fear of fire and seamen would live for weeks on cold food rather than risk a hot ember pitching from a modest galley fire in bad weather. The thought of a large steam boiler furnace and funnel sparks must have appeared quite ludicrous at the time. However, the attractions of a power-driven vessel were very powerful in themselves and serious attempts were made from at least 1736 when Jonathon Hulls published his design for a stern paddle wheeler up to 1786 when John Fitch ran a steamboat on the Delaware, 1788 when Patrick Miller ran another and so on until the famous paddle steamer *Clermont* in 1807 started running the first commercial steam packet service on the Hudson. She, it is worth noting, was 133 feet in length with the very narrow beam of 13 feet and her 20 nominal horse-power engine drove her at a trial speed of 3·7 knots. She transmitted her engine power into forward propulsion with two fifteen-feet diameter paddle wheels each four feet wide.

Although the basic principles of the screw propeller had been known since antiquity, it was natural at the time to apply the familiar techniques of the water wheel to the new situation, where the power and the water speeds were directly comparable. Even with the advance in engine output power through the years the paddle wheel remained a favourite method of power propulsion for more than a century—particularly when allied to the steam engine.

The first reasonably successful trials of a man-powered screw propeller were carried out in Gibraltar Bay as early as 1802 to test a patent taken out by Edward Shorter for a 'perpetual sculling machine'. A windmill-like device was fixed in the water aft of the vessel and connected through a universal joint to a capstan when eight-man muscle power produced a speed of over a knot. Fitch and Fulton had also previously tried various screw propeller arrangements but in 1804 Colonel John Stevens demonstrated a twin screw vessel at speeds up to 7 or 8 mph. As his craft, the *Little Juliana,* was less than 25 feet in length such speeds meant that she was in fact driven just about as fast as she would go.

Power craft therefore began to nibble at the lure of speed, and hull form to suit the power began to creep into the considerations. Of course, it had been known to seamen probably since the beginning of time that fast craft were long and thin and light. More, they were also fine lined with sharp bows and delicate sterns. The fastest rowing craft, the river eights, were shaped thus and the fastest sailing craft, like the East coast beach yawls, showed the same characteristics. It was therefore logical, once the sheer functioning of the power unit could be assumed, to lengthen and fine the hull forms to increase the potential speed.

Since there was not, at that time, enough power available to blast the whole hull out of the water to achieve the planing state of skimming over the surface of the sea, the early power craft had to search for top speed in the so-called displacement state of travelling through the water. Here energy is required to push the water aside and to overcome the friction of the skin of the craft as it travels. The former, known as wave making, sets up a system of related waves, bow waves, etc. all along the hull to the stern wave. The extent and number of these depends on the speed and the length of the hull. In general the limiting condition which determines the maximum speed of a hull travelling in this displacement mode is the point at which the wave system is reduced to a total of two, bow and stern, with the hull just leaving the latter behind. Now the hull is without any aft support to keep it trimmed nearly level and is condemned to run for ever up the, by now, quite heavy slope of the bow waves. The power required to go faster rises to an almost impossible amount and any further increase in performance is impracticable without enormous power reserves. As the wave system is related to the length of the hull the two benefits of narrow beam to reduce the waves made and long length to delay the onset of the limiting speed can be seen on nearly every early power craft with pretensions to speed.

The development of small lightweight steam engines allowed their installation in small lightweight boats and for these to be driven quite fast. In particular Nathaniel Herreshoff, the American designer, developed a style of fast launch specially for the sheltered waters of Long Island Sound in the 1870s. These beautifully built craft were extremely light, often double ended, and with screw propellers often reached speeds of twenty knots. Although these launches were often used for commuting to business in the City of New York there is little doubt that one of the principal attractions was just that of skimming over the sunlit seas at hitherto impossible speeds. Of course size increased as well as speed and from the pleasure craft developed some of the early torpedo boats. There is little lasting pleasure in going

right: The famous *Turbinia* ushers in the turbine age at a speed of 34 knots.

far right: Perhaps the most successful of the multi-stepped hydroplanes, *Maple Leaf IV* held the world speed record at 57 mph for several years up to 1920.

right: In the early years of this century there was a great deal of research done into many forms of faster power boating, including, for instance, this Grocco-Ricaldone hydrofoil built in 1906 by the famous Italian firm of Baglietto.

far right: The coastal motor boats of the first world war were developed directly from the hydroplane *Miranda IV*. This is one of the smaller ones.

yachting with a load of coal in a small fast wind-blown launch and so by about the 1880s a kind of steam engine was produced which used naphtha or paraffin as fuel instead of coal. The overall reduction in bulk also meant that engines could be fitted in small launches and even dinghies down to about twelve feet in length.

In 1884 Sir Charles Parsons patented the reaction steam turbine, which although now primarily connected with large and fast steamships was originally proved in small and even faster craft. The famous *Turbinia* which upset Queen Victoria's Diamond Jubilee Spithead review by steaming through the fleet at 34 knots was only a hundred feet in length and nine feet in beam, powered by three Parsons turbines totalling no less than 2,000 shaft horse-power. However, although steam turbines were built and installed in quite small craft they were, so far as really fast craft were concerned, overtaken by the internal combustion engine.

The first really successful internal combustion engine was J J E Lenoir's gas engine patented in 1860, and Dr Otto produced his first four-cycle engine in 1876, but the first internal combustion oil engine used successfully in a marine installation was a Priestman two-cylinder single-acting engine which was fitted in a 28-foot boat in 1888. Two years before, however, Gottlieb Daimler, the motor car pioneer, put the first recorded motor boat afloat. She was a small launch powered by a 1½-hp benzine motor. At the turn of the century there were a considerable number of petrol engines available from the rising car industry and of course it was natural to adapt them for boat use. The year 1900 saw a contest between the best steam-engined launch that Herreshoff could produce, the *Swiftsure*, and a motor boat called *Vingt-et-Un II*. The latter, with her 75-hp Panhard engine, won and effectively closed the era of fast steam launches.

In 1903, Sir Alfred Harmsworth, afterwards Lord Northcliffe, offered a cup for a fast power boat contest. The Harmsworth Trophy developed into an international contest of comparable standing and passions to the America's Cup trophy for sailing boats. The Harmsworth Trophy, later called the British International Trophy, was for the best of three heats each of between thirty and forty miles in length in craft under forty feet in length. The first race was held in the harbour of Queenstown (Cobh) and was won by *Napier I* owned by Mr S F Edge at a speed of 19·53 mph, the first recorded world water speed record.

The following year Mr Edge in a new boat, *Napier Minor*, 35 feet in length with a 55-hp Napier engine, again won the Harmsworth Trophy at 23½ mph against a field of nine boats from Britain, France and America. In the same year the first cross-Channel race was held from Calais to Dover and it is notable that of twenty-one starters only one boat failed to finish the course. The winner, *Mercedes IV*, covered the course in just over one hour, and the French destroyer acting as guard ship nearly burst her boilers keeping up with the tiny craft. In 1907 the Americans won the Harmsworth Trophy at a speed of 31 mph with *Dixie* and successfully defended it the following year with *Dixie II* which put up the world water speed record to 36 mph. She was an extreme example of her type with an overall length of the maximum allowed, 40 feet, and only 5-feet beam, low in the water and with rounded soft sections to her slender hull designed to pass through the water with the minimum of disturbance. The Duke of Westminster built a slightly larger craft called *Ursula* with the above-water bulk reduced to the minimum, and that extensively faired, to achieve over 40 mph.

The time of the long thin fine raceboat however was over for there was now power available to push boats up on top of the surface of the water where they could skim and plane along leaving most of the wave-making and a great part of the skin-friction drag behind them. After the ability to go straight into the eye of the wind the prospect of planing is the most important ability which the engine offers to boats. Free from the ploughing of furrows through the sea the boat becomes theoretically unlimited in speed, and in practice only limited by the prospect of going so fast that it becomes an aircraft. Furthermore it is a prospect which works its way upwards from the smallest craft. A ten footer is planing at twelve knots, a fifty footer at thirty knots, a hundred footer at 40 knots, whereas a thousand foot ocean liner would have to find enough power to do one hundred and thirty knots to reap the benefits.

Although a planing hull requires quite different characteristics of form for maximum efficiency at speed the shape of craft did not change abruptly. The power available to drive the craft up through her bow wave was at first only just sufficient and the toothpick form was eminently necessary in order to get the hull travelling fast enough even to start planing. The early planing craft therefore were not all that dissimilar from earlier boats except that they had nearly flat bottoms. As the power available increased so the regard for an efficient hull form for the speed range before planing decreased. The hull could be blasted through the difficult range and some consideration given to planing efficiency. This preferred rather short and wide planing bottoms and so the very fast boat tended to get shorter and boxier. The ideal planing shape in the 1930s for instance was a vee pointed bow which faired out as fast as it could to a flat or nearly flat bottom.

Planing of course brought a new set of problems to get over. First was the quite different cornering characteristics. The displacement craft heels out when turning, the planing boat, in. The planing boat turning at speed builds up considerable centrifugal force and therefore skids to a quite extensive degree. This causes the hull form, riding on top of the water surface, to plane

right: The last time the British International Trophy was raced for in British waters *Miss America* won it at a speed of 53 mph with 800 hp. Note the bow rudder.

opposite top: Saunders-Roe of Cowes built *Miss England II*. This picture shows the stepped bottom and the trouble taken to avoid structural discontinuity.

right: Miss England II after setting up a world water speed record of 110·28 mph at Lake Garda, Italy, in July 1931. Her overhanging transom arrangement is just coming back into fashion with modern power boats.

opposite bottom: The first boat to travel at two miles a minute: *Miss England III*, built by Thornycrofts and fitted with early Rolls Royce Merlin engines.

11

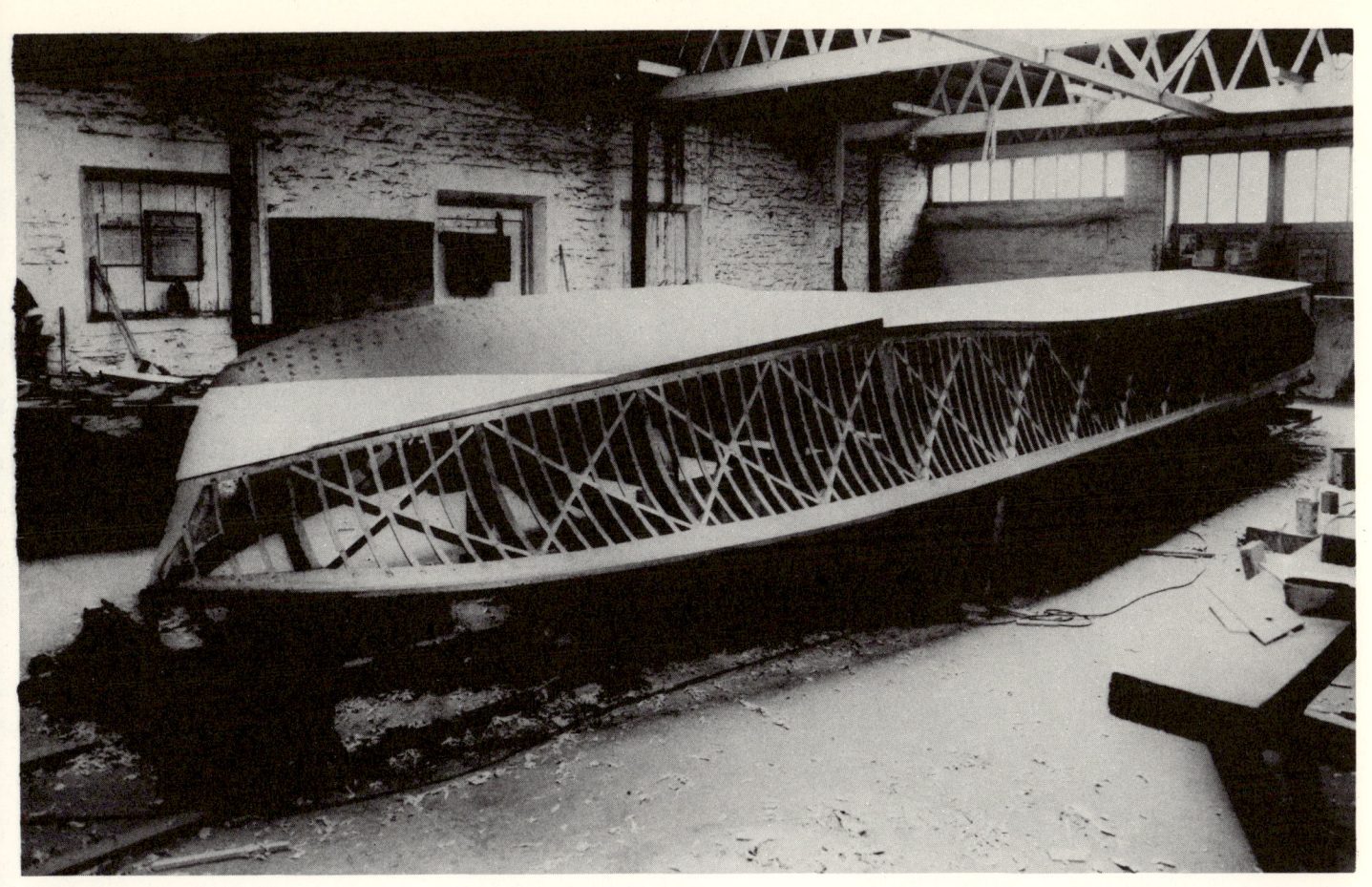

right: *Miss Britain III*, one of the most significant craft in the development of top speed power boat racing is now to be seen in the National Maritime Museum at Greenwich.

below: The first of the famous *Bluebirds* followed closely along the lines of *Miss Britain III* but was powered with a single Rolls Royce Merlin engine. This picture shows her on Loch Lomond in 1937.

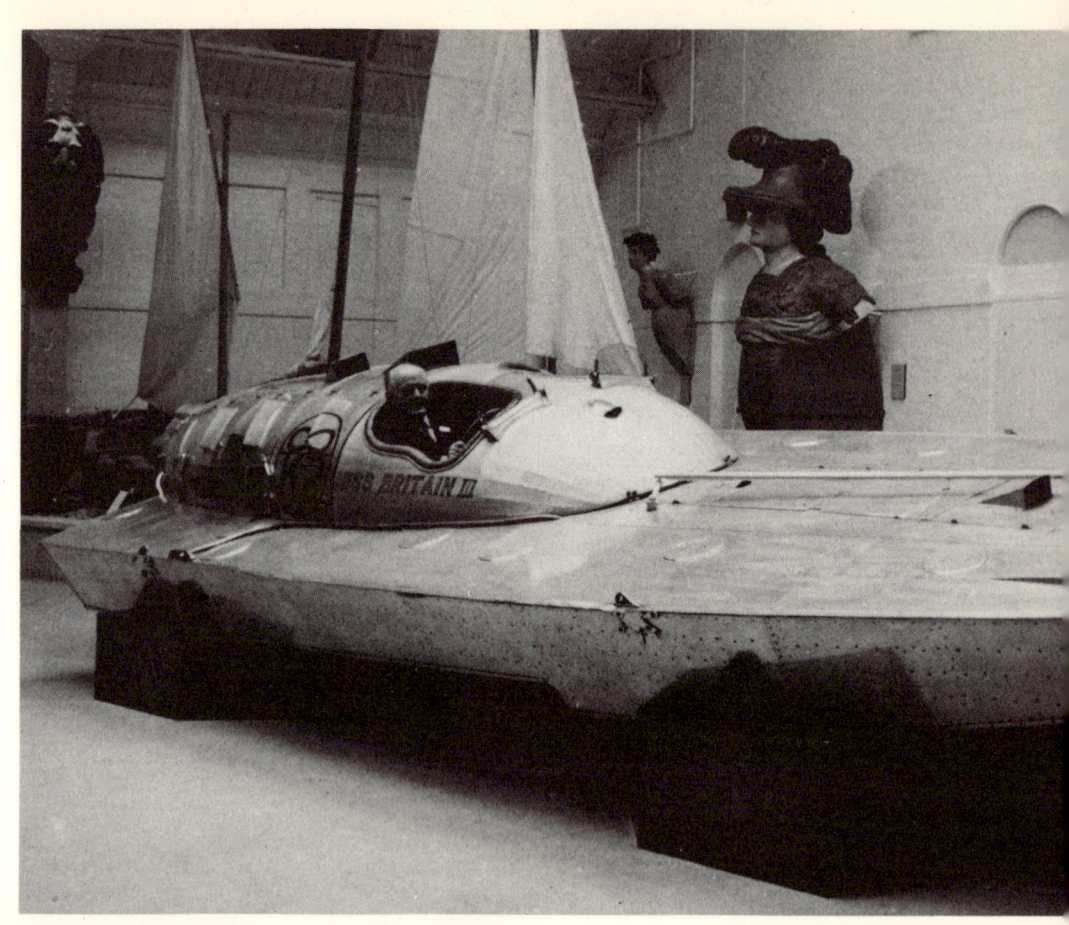

sideways as it turns and if the low lying chine should catch, or trip, the craft will capsize readily. This led to the development of the non-trip chine with its high raking edge to produce an anti-capsize moment during the turn. The next most important problem is that of so-called porpoising, where the planing boat builds up a rhythmic nodding motion which can range from the pleasant to the disastrous. Porpoising is due to the relationship of the hull weight centre of gravity and the planing surface. If the hull is powered out of the water to the point where the centre of gravity gets ahead of the planing area the hull weight will tip the bow down until it is again supported by the sea. The additional skin friction drops the hull speed, the craft settles and then builds up speed again to repeat the whole process again and again. A non-porpoising hull requires not only careful allocation of weights but considerable care in the shape of the actual planing surfaces to keep the hull trim at speed under control. The biggest bar to planing efficiency of the traditional long hull was the extent of the wetted surface. The stepped hull was developed with great success to reduce this aspect. Here the hull is built with two or more separate planing surfaces down its length separated by a vertical upwards gap called a step. This allowed each planing surface to be designed for efficiency without affecting the overall shape of the hull. Each step, however, in itself created a great deal of drag at speed unless it was given free access to suck air as the hull moved forward. Steps were therefore exaggerated in depth at the sides of the hull so that they could be properly ventilated from the edges. In rough water, however, such a step could be masked by a passing wave crest and the sudden increase in drag on one side could play havoc with the steering. In any case driving a thin boat with a great deal of engine torque and a bottom like a ski over the slippery water was a bit like driving a bicycle on ice and steering was often more a matter of judgement rather than control. In fact, the hydroplane, because of its speed and new characteristics was originally essentially a flat water craft.

The hydroplane boat, as it was called, had been a twinkle in the designer's eye, so to speak, since 1872 when the Rev. Ramus proposed the idea to the Admiralty. In 1877 Sir John Thornycroft even took out patents, but planing was not possible until the lightweight engines were developed (principally of course for the car and aeroplane) and adapted for marine use.

One of the first racing craft built as a pure hydroplane was the *Pioneer* built for the Duke of Westminster. She proved very fast and capable in fact of 45 mph. However, she failed to win the Harmsworth Trophy from the American *Dixie III* due to engine problems. The famous *Maple Leaf IV* regained the trophy in 1912 and raised the official world speed record to 43 mph. In 1913 she raised it again to 57 mph, a figure which stood all through the war period until 1920. *Maple Leaf IV* was powered with a 760-hp New Orleans engine and had a hull with no less than five steps along her length. It is worth noting that she was 40 feet in length but with a beam of 8 feet 5 inches compared for instance with the 5-feet beam of *Dixie II*.

13

below: Alagi, Italian holder of the world speed record before Sir Malcolm Campbell broke it in 1937. She was built by Baglietto and had a 12-litre Isotta Fraschini engine.

bottom: The three-pointer *Bluebird* built in 1939. This picture in fact shows her when reconverted to her original form for Donald Campbell in 1949. In this form she ran at up to 145 mph.

The famous shipbuilding firm of Thornycrofts had also taken a great interest in hydroplanes. Sir John Thornycroft, who had taken out some early patents, and his son Tom had produced in 1909 a craft called *Miranda III* followed next year by the particularly successful *Miranda IV* capable of speeds up to 40 mph. When the war broke out they developed a design of coastal motor boats based initially on *Miranda IV*. These were torpedo boats which launched their torpedoes astern into their wakes and then powered off out of the way. The first of these craft were only 40 feet long and capable of 35 mph. Later craft were bigger and faster with, for instance, the 55 footers capable of 45 mph. The coastal motor boats were essentially flat-water craft, very lightly built and with speed as their principal protection when delivering and retiring from a torpedo attack. They were wooden craft with forward and after steps built onto the basic hull after planking. Other countries, especially the Italians, also developed the hydroplane hull as a midget warship form. The war brought along fast the development of power units to suit the lightweight high output requirements of aircraft and so when power boat racing was recommenced after the war there was a whole new range of possibilities available.

There was no Harmsworth Trophy race in 1919 but in 1920 Commodore Garfield Wood won it for America with the first of his *Miss Americas* and set a new world water speed record of 61 mph. The speed was perhaps not a great increase on *Maple Leaf IV* but *Miss America* was of more advanced form with only 26 feet in length and 800 hp. She initiated a series of power boat races of remarkable excitement and interest and indeed of remarkable cost, making use of the high technology light engines coming from the aircraft industry. The Americans, led by Commodore Wood, and the British took different paths to high speed. The Americans went in for maximum power, cramming each craft with as much power as it could carry. The British went for efficiency and powered quite lightweight and small craft with a single or twin engines to achieve comparable power/weight ratios and speeds. This was the beginning of the famous contests between the *Miss Americas* and the *Miss Englands*.

Miss America II raised the world speed record to 80 mph in 1921 and in 1928 *Miss America VII* raised it again to 92 mph. However, she was beaten boat for boat round the course by a remarkable new craft called *Miss England* designed by Fred Cooper and built by Hubert Scott-Paine. Compared with the 2,300 hp of *Miss America VII* she was powered only with a single Napier Lion engine of 930 hp and yet had a speed of over 90 mph. Further she was much more manoeuvrable and Sir Henry Segrave, her pilot, was therefore much quicker at turning. In his efforts to avoid loosing ground at the corners of the course Commodore Wood strained and broke the steering gear of *Miss America VII*.

The next British boat, *Miss England II*, also designed by Fred Cooper but built by Saunders Roe of Cowes, was only 32 feet long and fitted with two Rolls-Royce engines of 1,900 hp each. Sir Henry Segrave made two runs at Lake Windemere in 1930 and established a world speed record of 98 mph, one of his two runs being over the 100 magic figure. Tragically, the very next run, when travelling even faster, the craft hit a log which tore away the forward step and rolled her over. Sir Henry Segrave and one of her two mechanics were drowned. The next year, in 1931, Commodore Wood in *Miss America VIII* raised the speed record to 102 mph.

Miss England II's story was far from over. She was raised, reconditioned, and Kaye Don took her to the Argentine where in difficult water conditions he raised the record to 103 mph and in the same year went to Italy and raised it still further to 110 mph. Again, in the same year, she faced *Miss Americas VIII* and *IX* in the Harmsworth Trophy and although clearly the better boat in speed and manoeuvrability in the first race, was tricked into a false start in the second and capsized. In 1932 Commodore Gar Wood again raised the record, this time to 111 mph.

Miss England III was built by Thornycrofts, 35 feet in length and fitted with two Rolls-Royce engines of 2,000 hp each. She, too, was sponsored by Lord Wakefield and put the *Miss Englands* back on top for a while. In 1932 she became the first boat to travel at two miles a minute and raised the world speed record to 119 mph. When taken to America for the Harmsworth Trophy, however, she was matched against the latest and indeed the tenth and last *Miss America*. She was a veritable marine monster with her 38 feet of length filled with no less than four Packard engines totalling 6,400 hp. Surprisingly it was *Miss England III* who had installation trouble in the race and Commodore Wood retained the trophy. Shortly afterwards he set up a speed record of 124 mph which stood for five years until Sir Malcolm Campbell arrived with the *Bluebird* series of craft.

One other raceboat of the time deserves a mention and this is the remarkable *Miss Britain III* built by Scott Paine in 1933. This beautiful tiny craft, only 24 feet in length, was powered by a single Napier Lion engine rated at 1,370 hp. She was part built and clad in aluminium and was very distinctive with her streamlined aircraft type engine cowling with twin cockpits. She proved very nearly as fast around the course in an apparently unequal Harmsworth Trophy contest as *Miss America X* in 1933 although the latter now sported a power output of no less than 7,800 hp. In 1934 she set up a world record for single engined craft of 110 mph at Genoa and proved conclusively that the future of fast boats lay along her line rather than with the sheer brute force approach of the *Miss Americas*.

Record breaking now really got into the hands of the professionals and the specialists. Public interest, fame and indeed fortune, all lay with the magical top figures. Hydroplane racing continued as one branch of the sport with the Harmsworth Trophy and Gold Cup contests in America but record making became a very specialised art accomplished with boats built especially for the purpose and practically unsuitable for anything else. The major British drivers in the latter end of the Harmsworth Trophy series, like Sir Henry Segrave and Kaye Don, had originated in car racing. Now Sir Malcolm Campbell at the age of fifty took up the quest for maximum speed over water.

The first of the famous *Bluebirds* was a single step hydroplane designed by Fred Cooper and built by Saunders Roe of Cowes in 1936. She was 24 feet in length and generally very like *Miss Britain III* but powered with a single Rolls-Royce engine of 2,500 hp. In 1937 on Lake Maggiore she broke Gar Wood's record with a speed of 126 mph and in the same year and place further increased it to 129 mph. Next year Malcolm Campbell raised it again to 130 mph in Switzerland, but this had just about stretched the boat to its limit and in fact had just about explored the two-stepped hull to its limit as well.

It was about this time that an American designer, Arno Apel, was building three pointer hulls, taking the next step forward in the logical development of the very fast craft. In the three pointer all pretence and tradition of the displacement hull and the previous feelings towards some rough water performance were abandoned for a logical look at high speed travel skimming over water. The previous two-stepped hulls at top speed in fact balanced on two tiny planing surfaces one behind the other. Arno Apel put these planing surfaces into a logical arrangement with the two forward areas widely separated for stability and the third aft on the centreline. This gave the craft an enormous basic stability when running and allowed each planing surface to operate in virtually undisturbed water. Sir Malcolm Campbell asked Peter Du Cane of Vospers to design and build him a new, three pointer, *Bluebird* in 1939. The new boat looked strange to the eye, but fitted with the old Rolls-Royce engine from the first *Bluebird*, performed extremely well and immediately raised the speed record to 141 mph.

The same year saw the outbreak of the Second World War and the end of record breaking and racing for some years. The lessons of the Thornycroft coastal motor boats in the first war appeared to have been quickly forgotten. The only fast midget warships built between the wars in Britain were built as private enterprises in 1936 and 1937 by Vospers to the design of Peter Du Cane, and the British Power Boat Company to the design of Scott-Paine. Both of these were simple unstepped hulls of about 70 feet in length and capable of speeds between 30 and 40 knots depending on the armament. In fact hundreds were built through the war period but the First World War idea of speed for its own sake was replaced with a greater requirement for performance in rougher sea conditions and a full defensive armament. The greater number were built as torpedo boats but a surprisingly large number were built as gunboats. Their function was to raid coastal shipping and to engage in battles with their German and Italian opposite numbers in fast moving fleet actions where hostile craft approached at combined speeds up to 80 mph. A typical craft of the period was 70 feet long and fitted with three Packard aero-type engines developing 4,500 hp total, driving three propellers to give a speed of about 36 knots.

opposite top: The second *Bluebird* converted to jet propulsion with her De Havilland Goblin engine.

opposite bottom: The first of the record breaking prop-riders, *Slo-Mo-Shun IV*, runs with her aft end supported only by the propeller.

below: John Cobb's jet powered *Crusader* used a three-ski arrangement with the single ski forward.

below: Donald Campbell's final *Bluebird* used two running ski surfaces forward and one aft. The plates under the hull are to reduce spray thrown up into the jet intakes at low speeds.

opposite: Gay Bombardier, typical of small fast patrol boats essentially derived from fast power yachts and raceboats.

Again a war situation urged along the development of a whole range of technology ready and waiting to be applied to even faster power boats after the war. Chief among the advances in propulsion was, of course, the development of the jet engine. Sir Malcolm Campbell was very enthusiastic about its potential for marine use and, instead of looking for modest speed advances with piston engines, decided to have *Bluebird* converted to jet propulsion. Peter Du Cane, her designer, planned an installation for a De Havilland Goblin jet and redesigned the whole superstructure. The new version of the three pointer *Bluebird* looked quite different with a highly streamlined appearance with twin jet inlets either side of the cockpit.

In 1947 the revised *Bluebird* went to Coniston and all seemed set for a new record. However, all did not go well. The boat proved to be quite uncontrollable at speeds over 80 mph and was taken back to Vospers for modification. These greatly improved her but at some 120 mph she ran into a phase of violent pitching or seesawing movements. Before she could be further modified Sir Malcolm died and the *Bluebird* story was taken over by his son Donald. De Havillands were not keen on an inexperienced driver handling a jet in an unproved boat and asked for their engine back and Bluebird was reconverted to her original piston engine installation and superstructure. In this form she made several runs up to 145 mph but at top speed showed a tendency to lift her stern.

In America a most remarkable boat had been developed by Stanley Sayers. *Slo-Mo-Shun IV* was a tiny light craft fitted with a single Allison petrol engine of 1,500 hp. She was not only capable of making a world record speed of 160 mph but also of taking part in and winning the Harmsworth Trophy races. What was most remarkable about her was that she had abandoned the aft planing surface and relied on the propeller itself for the necessary lift. The propeller of tiny size rotating at 3,300 rpm produced enough power to lift itself until the boss was at the water surface and the propeller blades working half in and half out of the water each rotation. This phenomena, known as prop riding, eliminated the skin friction of the after step and also the drag of the propeller shaft which now ran dry and clear of the water surface at speed. It was in fact an element of this effect which was causing the aft end of *Bluebird* to lift and thereby spoil her performance. As soon as this became understood *Bluebird* was completely rebuilt to become a prop-rider and although she performed satisfactorily in this style she never actually regained her record. On her last attempt she was running up towards 170 mph when she hit a log and sank. Although she was recovered the hull itself was wrecked beyond repair.

The next contender for the record stakes was John Cobb. Stanley Sayers had raised the record to 178 mph in 1952 but Cobb was aiming at speeds of over 200 mph with a Goblin-powered craft of revolutionary design. *Crusader* was designed by Peter Du Cane to run supported by a bow planing surface and two water-ski-like floats spaced either side of the jet engine aft. While travelling at nearly 240 mph she developed a porpoising motion of great speed and intensity and disintegrated, killing her driver. Two years later the Italian pilot Mario Verga met with a similar disaster and was killed on Lake Iseo in his boat *Laura 3a*.

Donald Campbell, however, started on the design work for yet another *Bluebird*.

Now that boats were travelling faster than some aircraft the aerodynamics of the design work were quite as important as the hydrodynamics. One of the problems in fact was to stop the craft aeroplaning. A delicate balance had to be arranged between an aerodynamic flow over the hull which would keep it down on the surface and the need to keep the loading on the planing surfaces to the minimum. At speeds over 200 mph a tiny change in such balance can send the boat flying off the surface to disaster since landing on water at such speeds is not very much different from landing on concrete.

The new *Bluebird* was to be propelled by a Beryl jet and was to follow some of the thinking of *Crusader*. She was to be fitted with two sponson floats but forward and not aft and her third support point was to be the aft end of the main hull, in fact the same three point disposition that was originally designed for the previous craft. In 1955 she became the first boat to travel at more than 200 mph and started a long run of record breaking. By 1964, now fitted with an Orpheus jet engine, she had raised the world speed record for boats to 276 mph. In 1967 while travelling at an estimated 300 mph *Bluebird* took off and crashed back, smashing herself and killing Donald Campbell.

The grand part of record breaking was over and public interest which had been declining in an age of supersonic travel more or less evaporated. With spacemen travelling at unimaginable speeds to the moon, pure velocity lost its appeal and the great interest in fast sea travel moved on to competitive racing again.

Power for Luxury Craft

The Royal paddle yacht *Elfin*, built of mahogany in Chatham in 1848.

Why should a gentleman take to power yachting? Certainly the original answer to such a question was that there was every reason why he should not and no reason why he should. The steam vessel had an element of danger from fire and explosion and was full of smoke, coal and machinery all of which had little to do with pleasure afloat. Speed and reliability were not important in the 1820s and even years later it was confidently remarked, 'Some yacht owners aim at speed but as a general rule fast passages are not required and it is natural that when one goes to sea for pleasure a speedy return is seldom required'.

In 1827 the Royal Northern Yacht Club as part of their general regatta celebrations went so far as to present a cup, value twenty guineas, for the 'swiftest steamboat' around a course in the Clyde. The race was a pure novelty but a noted yachtsman of the time, Mr T Assheton Smith, was sufficiently attracted to think of having a steam boat built for himself. He even suggested that such vessels might be admitted to the (Royal) Yacht Squadron. Such impudence met with a broadside, as witness this resolution passed by the Yacht Squadron in Thatched House Tavern in the same year: 'that as a material object of this club is to promote seamanship and the improvements of sailing vessels, to which the application of steam engines is inimical, no vessel propelled by steam shall be admitted into the club and any member applying a steam engine to his yacht shall be disqualified thereby and cease to be a member'.

Mr Assheton Smith, although no doubt shaken, resolved to go ahead and ordered a craft to be built for the sum of £20,000. The *Menai*, as she was called, was completed in 1830 as the first recorded steam yacht. This historic craft was a paddle wheeler of about 120 feet in length and 20 feet beam. Mr Smith was obviously pleased with her for he had no less than eight more steam yachts built over the next twenty years. One of these was capable of speeds of up to sixteen knots and one was an experimental screw steamer.

In 1844 the Royal Yacht Squadron relaxed its views so far as to admit yachts of not less than 100 hp to the benefits and privileges and indeed by 1853 they removed all restrictions. The steam yacht was respectable and could consider itself as a fully acceptable appurtenance to the existence of a gentleman. It is possible to believe that the Noble Lords in their headquarters at Cowes were a little influenced by the construction in Pembroke in 1843 of a 200-foot paddle yacht named *Victoria and Albert* for Queen Victoria.

Paddle yachts in fact were very popular with the Royal family who made extensive use of them between the mainland and Osborne House in the Isle of Wight. In 1845 the *Fairy*, an iron built screw yacht of 146 feet in length was built as a tender to the *Victoria and Albert* but only three years later the *Elfin*, a wooden paddle yacht, was built for the same job. Indeed the 160-foot *Alberta*, another wooden paddle yacht, was built specifically to replace the *Fairy* in 1863 and the poor old *Fairy* was actually recorded as being 'taken to pieces'. *Victoria and Albert* herself was replaced by a bigger yacht in 1855 and in 1870 the last of the paddle-wheeled Royal yachts, the *Osborne*, was built. She was a large vessel of some 250 feet in length, although she looked modest beside the final *Victoria and Albert*, a 380-foot twin-screw steamer built in 1899.

Perhaps these Royal paddlers set a fashion, for steam yacht owners largely stuck to paddles until the 1870s, despite the obvious superiority of the screw not only for propulsive efficiency but in the accommodation layouts involved and, not least, in the use of the yacht with an auxiliary rig. All the early steamers put to sea with only semi-confidence in their power plants, and all, more or less without exception, carried a quite extensive outfit of masts and sails. A pair of paddle wheels, however, is an embarrassment to a sailing ship. The drag, even when sailing upright, is formidable and at an angle of heel the lee paddle would be as good as an anchor and very vulnerable to damage when immersed beyond its axis. All manner of interesting devices were tried in order to make the paddle wheel 'sail' including great wooden fairing floats strapped around them and elaborately folding wheels. These were rarely successful and it is odd that the obvious advantages of the screw did not become appreciated until *Sunbeam* was built for Lord Brassey in 1874. She, it is true, was a large sailing vessel which only used her screw when the wind did not serve but her evident success gave a great impetus to the use of the screw in general for yacht propulsion.

While the sheltered Long Island Sound in America became the leading area for fast launches, it is the Clyde which became world renowned for steam yachts. This was partly a spin-off from its growing reputation for shipbuilding and marine engine making, but the neighbouring West coast of Scotland must have formed the ideal cruising ground for steam yachts. At about the same time the Victorian industrial revolution was spinning wealth and many landowners were building themselves large and elaborate houses as shooting lodges in remote parts of Scotland. These were invariably on the lochside as the roads of the time were practically impossible. Building materials and labour were shipped in by sea from Glasgow and Fort William and in due course the owner and his guests arrived by steam yacht. The yacht in fact was the only practical method of conveyance and a steam yacht generally served as a tender to each shooting lodge.

The steam yacht also covered the ground at a great rate. At eight knots some 200 miles can be run in each day with great reliability. This not only meant that the industrial tycoon could rely, much more than hitherto, on keeping to his schedules but also that in his month's holiday he could cruise much further afield. The steam yacht in effect spread to the Mediterranean where it was found to be ideal for the local conditions. In an area which alternates between light winds and strong blows the steam yacht can slip along the Riviera coast from golden port to golden port in ideal conditions and scarcely an interruption to the sybaritic life on board. Further, the fast train service from the Channel ports direct to the Mediterranean meant that owner and guests did not themselves have to take the seagoing passage down the Atlantic coast and past Gibraltar to get to their yachting ground.

The Victorian yachtsman was not only rich and growing richer but he lived in a time when iron, steam power, electricity, and the 'manufactures' had upset all preconceived ideas on what was or was not possible. All manner of quite fundamental beliefs were now questioned and every aspect of boating appeared quite capable of improvement. Several marine oddities were built to test out various new theories but perhaps the oddest in yachting was the Russian Imperial circular yacht *Livadia*. Yachts of the day were generally narrow in beam and fitted with a quite extensive outfit of masts and spars for auxiliary sails. They therefore rolled heavily both at sea and on moorings unless the sea was quite flat. Anyone who has experienced such rolling will appreciate any attempt to reduce it. John Elder, a Glasgow shipbuilder, argued that it was narrow beam that was the culprit and that therefore rolling could be completely eliminated if the hull was, say, circular in plan. There was something of a craze for circular yachts for a short time and among those convinced of the argument was the Russian Admiral Popov. He saw a stable gun platform in the idea and had a circular battleship built. The *Admiral Popov*, as the ship herself was named, was not a great success and tended to spin rather than move ahead when her eight screws were given power. However, the idea also attracted Czar Alexander who had the circular *Livadia* built for him in Glasgow in 1880. The lower part of the hull, 235 feet long with a beam of 153 feet, was more turbot shaped than anything else with a slightly more conventional superstructure on top of it. This topside area contained the crew's quarters with the Royal suites in deckhouses above. She required no less than 10,000 hp to reach 15 knots and must have been an extraordinary and impressive sight with her three funnels set athwartships. It is reported that she was remarkably free from rolling in the small seas of the Baltic but that in heavy weather rolling was scarcely diminished.

Rolling, in fact, was one of the problems with the screw steamer. The paddler gained a certain amount of stabilisation from the damping effect of her wheels but the same hull fitted with a screw rolled freely. The problem was partly engine efficiency and partly historical. A sailing ship is largely damped from rolling by the pressure of the winds on her sails which act as large air stabilisers. At the same time the masts and spars were a fairly delicate erection and sailing ships were designed to roll slowly and easily. A sharp roll from a very stable hull form could give the rigging a whip action which could bring it down. The early steamers were in effect converted sailing ships complete with all or some of their rig and had to set steadying canvas at sea. As the engines became more reliable and the auxiliary sailing rig an anachronism the latter tended to disappear leaving a hull which was long and thin for performance and without any real stabilisers.

Rolling in fact remained something of a problem until the advent of the power stabiliser fins in the last few years. The seaman, possibly with atavistic memories or a training in sail, liked his ship to roll easily and did not mind if it rolled far. The non-seaman, who might be the owner, was generally alarmed by the amplitude and preferred a quick roll which reassured him of the hull's stability. As the heavy rigs declined and disappeared their weight and windage required some form of compensation and it is interesting to see how deckworks and funnels grew. The tall thin funnel originally required to give a good draught to the boiler fires was replaced by shorter and fatter funnels until the function of the smoke stack was as much to act as an air stabiliser as it was to carry away the smoke.

By the turn of the century the steam yacht, its development encouraged by the world's monarchs and the industrial millionaires, had become magnificent. Fine fast ships of a thousand tons were common, beautifully finished and maintained in fact to a quite extraordinary and almost impractical degree of perfection. The absurdity of sparkling white enamel in a coal burning vessel and of polished brass in a corrosive marine environment served, it must be thought, as much to demonstrate the owner's opulence as anything else. It was perhaps also a by-product of the absentee owner. A steam yacht would have a crew of twenty or thirty who had little to do between the owner's month-long visits but to titivate and polish and compete in finish with other yachts.

One of the most magnificent and luxurious was the steam yacht *Lysistrata* built by Denny of Dumbarton from designs of G L Watson for James Gordon Bennett of the United States. She was 286 feet long with 40 feet beam and a speed of 19 knots. Unlike most of her contemporaries she had a straight stem rather than a clipper or fiddle bow, probably in the interests of speed. One of the most famous yachts of the period was the *Rovensha* built by the Leith firm of Ramage and

left: The circular yacht was an attempt to improve comfort on board by reducing rolling. This example, the *Livadia*, was built in Glasgow for Czar Alexander in 1880.

below: The 160-foot wooden paddle wheel yacht *Alberta*, built for Queen Victoria in 1863 and used up to 1913.

bottom: The German yacht and despatch vessel *Kaiseradler*, built in 1876, on a visit to the Solent.

Ferguson in 1904. This yacht was renamed *Elettra* when she was bought by Marconi and in her the great inventor made many of his most important experiments. She was 220 feet long by 28 feet beam and was a particularly pretty vessel with an elegant fiddle bow.

Another yacht with a long and interesting career was the famous *Liberty*, well known latterly as the property of Dame Lucy Houston. The yacht, a twin-screw steamer, was built in 1908 at a cost of £270,000 for a blind American who sold her in 1912 to a Canadian who renamed her *Glencairn*. The following year she was bought back to Britain by Lord Tredegar who gave her back her original name. She served as a hospital ship through the First World War with her noble owner in command as a Captain RNVR. At the end of the war she was refitted and sold to Sir Robert Houston who used her for political cruises and on his death Lady Houston used her as headquarters for her own political and philanthropic work. The yacht was not broken up until 1938.

The First World War of course saw a great many yachts used for Admiralty service as hospital ships and despatch craft, even minesweepers. After the war yacht building started again but on a somewhat smaller scale and with a strong swing away in appearance from the tall thin stove pipe chimneys, fiddle bows, sweeping sheers and long counters which made the Victorian yacht the criterion for appearance right up to the present day. The immediate post-war years saw a positively commercial appearance with straight stems and cruiser sterns in fashion. This dull period was however enlivened by the appearance of the destroyer yacht. During the war these fast and lively craft caught a great many imaginations and after the war several yachts were built to look and behave like destroyers and

left: The famous yacht *Liberty*, typical of the pre-First World War steam yachts, and particularly well known when she was owned by Dame Lucy Houston.

below: Between the wars the tradition of the magnificant steam yacht was carried on by such vessels as the *Nahlin* of 1574 tons.

25

indeed torpedo boats. One of the best known of these was the *Cutty Sark*, built in 1920 by Yarrow and reputed at the time to be the fastest yacht afloat. She was 273 feet long with only 25 feet beam and, powered by four steam turbines, she could raise a speed of 24 knots. She was built for Major Keswick and was afterwards purchased by the Duke of Westminster.

In the 1930s yacht design began to swing away from the merchant or warship appearance into two main lines. The first was a reversion to Victorian/Edwardian appearance as represented by the well-known steam turbine *Nahlin* built in 1930 at a cost of a quarter of a million pounds for Lady Yule by John Brown of Clydebank, builders of the famous Queen liners. Among those who cruised in *Nahlin* was, of course, the then Prince of Wales. In 1937 she was sold to King Carol of Rumania and became the Royal yacht *Luceafarul*.

The other main line in a sense was coming up from the smaller power boats and two yards in the south of England particularly became famous for modern-looking diesel yachts. Thornycrofts and Camper & Nicholsons between them translated the romantic appearance of the large yacht into the motor yacht age. A bow with only a hint of the clipper about it was connected to a drawn-out cruiser-type stern by a flattish sheer. Deckworks were quite large and topped with a squat powerful-looking funnel. In general they were smaller than the great steam yachts but, thanks to the smaller engines and bunkers, the accommodation was probably much the same in extent. The Thornycroft classic series of *Trenora, Amazone, Gulzar* and *Tadorna* were about 130 feet in length and 21 feet beam and, with about 600 hp of diesel engines, had a speed of 12 or 13 knots and a range of 3/4,000 miles. In every way these were thoroughly satisfactory little ships capable of cruising the world. With such a range it was quite possible for them to winter in the West Indies and summer in the Mediterranean as a matter of course.

The classic example of Camper & Nicholsons' yacht building art of the period was *Philante* built in 1937 for Mr T O M Sopwith, the aircraft pioneer and America's Cup contender. *Philante* was one of the largest yachts afloat when she was built and was the largest British built motor yacht. She was twin-screw with twin MAN engines of 1,500 hp each, 263 feet in length with 38 feet beam and a top speed of 17 knots. After the war she was bought by the Norwegians to become the Royal yacht *Norge*.

Times change and so do the various pressures which decide the characteristics of yachts. Steam, for instance, was a power plant eminently suited to yachting so long as labour was cheap. Steam was quiet, the biggest blessing anyone can give a yacht, and it was warm, the second biggest blessing you can give a north European yacht. However, it was cumbersome and dirty, coal made dust and the fire made soot and the whole engine and its various associated equipment and bunkers took up a great deal of space. This did not matter too much so long as you could run a large crew to clean and stoke and so on. As labour costs increased the oil-fired boiler alleviated the situation for a while, but soon the cost of running a steam engine, when measured in labour and the space occupied by crew and machinery combined, began to overtake sense. Conversion to diesel engines was slow at first because the slow-running engines set up a general vibration and the smell of diesel oil was agreed to be unpleasant. Installation techniques of course improved and objections were overcome and the small steam yacht altogether ceased construction in the 1930s. Since the last war the diesel engine has been a major power plant for yachts of all sizes.

left: After the First World War there was a passing fancy for yachts which had a martial look. The Duke of Westminster owned *Cutty Sark,* reputed at the time to be the fastest yacht afloat with her speed of 24 knots.

opposite: The steam yacht *Elettra*, in which Marconi made many of his famous experiments, is now preserved as a museum ship in Italy.

below: A small Solent motor yacht, *Tamahine*, showing the general concentration on seaworthiness typical of the period before the Second World War.

bottom: Maureen Mhor, built in 1961 by Yarrows, is typical of the eminently seaworthy yachts built for northern waters.

opposite: The modern motor yacht was developed by Camper & Nicholsons and by Thornycrofts; *Philante* was one of the largest yachts afloat when she was built by Campers in 1937. She is now the Norwegian Royal yacht *Norge*.

In the years between the wars a most interesting breed of small yachts came onto the scene. Mostly they still stemmed in origin from the Clyde where the family sized motor yacht was ideal for holiday cruising around the Western Isles. These comparatively small yachts of sixty or seventy feet in length were excellent seaboats and cruised with the owner as captain, assisted by his family and possibly by a single paid hand who was responsible more for the maintenance of the craft rather than for her navigation. This kind of vessel was essentially the motor boat equivalent of the cruising sailing yacht and was used for what is called 'serious' cruising all over the northern coasts of Europe. The accommodation was simple rather than lavish and depended on the craftsmanship of the joiner for quality.

A typical example of the type was the Clyde yacht *Jester* built by James Silver. She was 68 feet in length with 15 feet beam and had speed of over 9 knots and a range of 700 miles. The Solent equivalent was perhaps the 63-foot *Tamahine* designed by Laurent Giles and built by Vospers in 1934. She had a speed of 12 knots with twin Gleniffer 120-hp diesels. Both yachts looked quite different from the Victorian ideals and owed more to the large motor yacht styling and current ideas on the shapes of merchant ships. Seamanship was, in fact still is, taken very seriously by the owners of such craft and the appearance of the yachts reflected this with an air of seagoing confidence and ability.

The Dutch developed a considerable reputation in this period for steel construction and built many fine yachts, and especially gained a name for yachts of about a hundred feet and under. Steel work in this size has to be done with great craftmanship if the yacht is not going to be overburdened with the weight of metal and cement fairing. The Dutch are world masters of this art and their skills before the war were exemplified by the yacht *Piet Hein*, which the people of the Netherlands gave to Queen Juliana and Prince Bernhard as a wedding gift. She was built by G de Vries Lentsch Jr of Amsterdam for cruising the waterways and canals, and is just over 100 feet in length and 18 feet beam and fitted with twin eight-cylinder Stork diesel engines of approximately 100 hp each.

Another development was the so-called express yacht devoted to short duration high-speed passages. This was in fact an extension upwards of the speed boat. Petrol engines were almost invariably necessary to achieve the required power/weight ratio and so the express yacht was more popular in the colder climates such as northern Europe or the northern sea-board of the United States than in the hot areas. Petrol boats still have a very unenviable reputation for exploding after quite modest carelessness when a hot ambient temperature can assist the liquid to vaporise. One of the most noted builders of large express cruisers was Fr Lurssen of Vegesack. A typical vessel would be of about seventy feet in length, built of wood and aluminium alloy, and, with three 420-hp petrol engines, would have a speed of about 34 knots.

Yacht Design Round the World

Mercury, who must be the fastest yacht of her size yet built, at her full, 50 knot, speed.

In these days of highly competitive sailing yachting, widely reported and discussed in the press, it is often difficult to recall that this is only the sporting end of yachting. Real yachting is intended, by definition, to be exclusively linked to pleasure. In sporting yachting passions can get high and great cornucopias of money often get spent on minor bits of machinery to save some semi-second across some imaginary finishing line. Real yachting can also cost money and many a handsome and imposing argosy gives pleasure to its owner as a marine palace or playboy pad of extensive sybaritic luxury. A modest, even simple, craft however is equally entitled to the label of yacht for giving her owner her own brand of delight in her ownership.

The roots of pleasure afloat lie, for most people, in confidence, and all the other edifices of pleasures get built on this basic framework. Confidence itself springs from a wide range of factors covering the seaworthiness of the hull, the state of the machinery, the reserves of fuel, the competence of the crew and so on. All these, however, are rooted in their background and related to the basic suitability of craft and crew for her cruising ground. Yachtsmen vary quite widely in their yachting requirements but it is clear that different yachting regions have developed significantly different types of yachts. Fashion, of course, exercises a big influence but behind superficial differences lie the basic characteristics which fashion has exaggerated.

In Great Britain the facts of yachting life start with a very modest amount of sheltered water, and none of it extensive enough or attractive enough to keep a yacht of any size captive all its life. Outside lie the choppy waters of the Channel, Irish and North seas. Atlantic winds blow across these shallow Continental shelf waters over strong tides, to kick up quick-rising short and high seas. The prevailing winds are westerly and, viewed from the sea, great lengths of the westerly coast of Britian and northern Europe are distinctly inhospitable as lee shores. Add to that seven delightful and interesting countries all within a few hundred miles and it is easy to see that the British yachtsman requires, above all, a good sea boat.

The beautiful *Woodpecker* displays the characteristics to perfection. Designed by Laurent Giles and built in 1948 she is, above everything else, a good sea boat, but showing how such a rather dull characteristic can be incorporated into a really beautiful craft, fully deserving all the inferences of grace and delicacy which go with the word yacht. *Woodpecker* is 70 feet long, powered by twin 100-hp diesels with accommodation only for the equivalent of two double cabins apart from her professional crew. In contrast to many later yachts she is not overfilled with accommodation and in special contrast to hot weather Mediterranean yachts she has extremely modest deckworks. *Woodpecker* is designed for open water cruising rather than hot weather harbour life.

Another yacht which illustrates the type is *Shandau*, designed by John Bain and Clyde built. She is 63 feet long and a little ship in every inch. Two 90-hp Gardner diesels give her a speed of 10 knots and she is laid out for family use, crewed and operated by her owners with only occasional professional assistance. Again compared with the yachts of more sheltered waters the freeboard is high and the deckworks concerned principally with the seagoing navigation of the vessel. A small funnel, in fact containing the water header tank, sets off the small ship appearance. It is perhaps indicative of the operating conditions anticipated when she was on the drawing board that she came out with a complete outfit of oil-fired central heating.

There is comparatively little to attract the Baltic yachtsman to leave his beautiful, extensive and protected waters. Beyond the Kattegat or the North Sea Canal is only a dull commercialised North Sea with fogs and rough water. The Baltic on the other hand is full of sheltered cruising grounds with literally thousands of protected anchorages within daily voyaging of each other. There is little need to make overnight passages and typically the Baltic motor yacht is small and beautifully finished. The large yacht traditions also typically stem from other yachting areas.

Around the rest of the North Sea coast only the Dutch with their vast inland waterways have developed a yachting industry of any consequence. Of course, with the North Sea between Holland and other cruising areas the essence of the Dutch yacht is again seaworthiness. The Dutch are also, thanks to an extensive demand for small inland waterway commercial craft, masters of small steel building.

Dutch yachts are immediately recognisable by their very 'shippiness', beautiful short-ended slightly stout craft brimming with seamanlike self-confidence. Typically, one might quote the 146-foot *Westlake III* built in 1966 to a de Vooght design by the famous builders C Van Lent & Zonen and fitted with twin 620-hp Deutz diesels. This magnificent yacht, large by any contemporary standards, was built for an American owner. An interesting illustration of the North Sea yacht subsequently re-built for the Mediterranean is *Rodi's Isle III* built by the Nieuwendam branch of the de Vries Lentsch yacht-building family in 1960 to a de Vooght design. She came out with only the most modest deckworks on top of her 100-foot hull but was re-built in Italy five years later for Mediterranean use, renamed *Together IV*. The reconstruction involved the building of a large on-deck saloon and galley and the replacement of a lavish below-deck accommodation based on two double cabins with no less than four small double cabins and a tiny single cabin. The handsome hull of this yacht shows off the canoe stern version of the big ship cruiser stern which is so suitable for a yacht of moderate speed. She was in fact designed to cruise at 13 knots, which is right at the top of the moderate speed band, and shows the elegant lines refined by tank testing to achieve it.

Faced with a choice of north or south coasts of France as a venue for their yachting, most French owners would naturally choose the Riviera. The Bay of Biscay was until comparatively recently a very fine area for sports fishing and a particular brand of seaworthy yachts developed along the Biscay coasts of France and Spain. The weather in the area is notorious, of course, and the Biscay yachts are necessarily of very seaworthy style. The Bay is some 200 miles across and the distance out to the fishing grounds makes a modest turn of speed desirable, so the typical yacht will probably have a speed of the order of fifteen knots and a range of 400 or 500 miles. A well-known pair of sister yachts, both built for Bay of Biscay champion sportsmen, are the 62-foot *Avila* and *Meche III*, built by Astilleros Udondo, the former for King Baudouin of the Belgians. These yachts again show relatively long slim easy hulls with only modest deckworks. They are powered by twin General Motors diesels and have accommodation for four guests in addition to their owners. It is again typical of the slightly working nature of a sports fishing yacht that the guest accommodation is in quite small cabins whose size in fact contrasts with a generally superb standard of fitting and finish throughout. It may be because wood is not an prolific material in Spain that the appreciation of it is so high and the craftsmanship of such a high order. Yachts like *Meche III* and *Avila* carry one or two fishing chairs on the aft deck and sport the long trolling rods typical of the commercial tunny fisherman.

The Atlantic coast of Spain and Portugal has few ports of refuge between Finisterre and the Tagus. The so-called Portuguese trades blow strongly for months at a time and there is little to attract other than the very dedicated cruising yacht or yachts on passage to the area. The Tagus however marks the start of southerly yachting. The Portuguese, surprisingly perhaps, do not have much of a yacht building industry. Many fine yachts are kept at Lisbon but they are almost exclusively imported craft. The south of Spain has a reasonable yachting area based on Cadiz where the more seaworthy of the Mediterranean craft can be seen. The great bulk of the world's large-yacht yachting however is concentrated through the straits of Gibraltar along the Riviera coastlines all the way from Spain to Greece.

A yacht which might be considered as a seaworthy example of the Mediterranean yacht is *Valvanera III* which in fact is owned near Cadiz and used frequently between Spain and Italy. She is a 90-foot, twenty-knot motor yacht built with a wooden hull, slightly unusual in her size, by Astilleros Udondo of Bilbao. She has accommodation with twin double guest cabins in addition to the owner's cabin, each of course with its own toilet compartment. She is fitted with twin Cummins twelve-cylinder vee engines and has fuel for five hundred miles. A yacht of this size will also carry, as she does, twin diesel generating plants capable of some twenty kilowatts of power. Her seaworthiness can again be noticed from the relatively modest deckworks over a big and powerful hull.

The Mediterranean in general and the Riviera coast in particular was, in the days before serious pollution and drastic overcrowding, the true home of the larger yacht for pleasure. The curious weather conditions really do not favour, to anything like the same degree, sporting yachting, but for a life of reasonably flat-water passage-making and week-long or even month-long lingers in exotic harbours they are ideal. The Mediterranean yachts can therefore be divided into two distinct groups. The first is the indigenous yacht, designed exclusively for the Mediterranean and even exclusively for the Riviera. Second are those yachts which come to the fleshpots from other ports and therefore have to be ocean-going, or the bigger and really international yachts which commute between the yachting grounds of the Mediterranean and, say, the West Indies at the owner's whim or on charter bookings. A third and not strictly relevant group can also be seen. These are yachts which are basicly unsuitable for all manner of reasons, old age being one of the most common, which are to be found more as semi-permanent homes. Scandinavian traders, Thames river yachts, government surplus warships, oversparred steam yachts—they are all to be seen mouldering away in Mediterranean ports, stirred only by unsympathetic harbour authorities who are increasingly bringing in regulations to require boats to put to sea once in a while, presumably to check if they actually do float and are not aground on the proverbial gin bottles.

The true Mediterranean native yacht from eastern Spain, France and especially from Italy, is usually an exotic vessel with style and elan, providing her owner with more of a luxurious extension to his shore life and fast car rather than a vehicle for practising seamanship. Speed is important in Italy, both for its own sake, but as also on account of the short weekends. A speed of

below: *Woodpecker*, with her long graceful hull and modest deckhouses shows to perfection how seaworthiness and yachting can be combined.

bottom: The 25-knot, 50-foot *Camanda* has the true luxury of little accommodation in a large hull.

right: Early power yachting was not universally popular. A steam launch on the Shire River in 1859.

far right: Hedonist, built by Camper & Nicholson, shows an open sea influence in her hull form.

Romantica with her dramatic bow also shows the extensive deckworks preferred for hot weather yachting.

34

35

twenty knots is necessary if the yacht is to reach further than the immediately neighbouring ports and return between Saturday lunchtime and Sunday evening. Flat-water slow-speed seamanship is dull if you are traversing the same area every weekend.

The yacht building company of Baglietto at Varezze is one of the best-known in Italy and epitomises in its craft the essence of Mediterranean sunshine yachting. Quite lightly built, powered with fast diesels, and well finished, they illustrate two facets of yachting different from that of the sun-starved North Sea. The last decade of styling has copied the aggressive appearance of the motor patrol boat with a quite introverted feeling to the accommodation. Partly this may be due to a desire for privacy when moored stern-on to the inevitably tightly packed marina or quay. Also, however, it must take some account of the excessive sunshine available on deck and look to small tinted windows for relief when inside. The Italians also lead the way in the decorative handling of the outside appearance of yachts. More than anyone else they feel free to build additional structure of little practical value just because it will look good. Appearance also dominates the shapes of windows, vents, flying bridges and paint areas, and although this may look a little profligate to Northern eyes, that it is the proper approach to vessels for pleasure there can be no doubt.

Many yachts are built all over the world designed and destined for Mediterranean use, making their way there on their own bottoms or sometimes on the deck of a ship. The 50-foot yacht *Camanda* was built for instance at Cowes, designed and built by a distinguished team of Raymond Hunt, Sir Hugh Casson and W A Souter & Son, for Mr Whitney Straight. She has the famous deep-vee hull form developed by Ray Hunt for fast and comfortable running at sea and is powered by a pair of eight-cylinder Cummins diesels giving a total power of over 700 hp and a speed of about 25 knots. Many

The 71-foot *Crest Cutter* shows how shelter from the sun becomes important for a Mediterranean yacht.

The 42-foot Hatteras convertible is entirely typical of the small, fast, American sports fishermen which make open sea passages out to the Gulf Stream.

yachts have a great deal of accommodation forced into them—accommodation is after all the pay load. *Camanda* however is another yacht in the grand manner with but a single double cabin for her owner in addition to the crew accommodation, saloon, galley and so on.

The British approach to sunshine yachting is shown also by the 83-foot fast motor yacht *Hedonist*, built by Camper & Nicholsons for the Hon Michael Pearson in 1969. She is, as her name implies, stuffed to the brim with luxury including her famous circular rotating bed. She shows a fairly typical Mediterranean type of deckworks with an aft canopy to act as sunshade for the on-deck life during the day. Her twin Cummins 12-cylinder diesels of 750 bhp each give her a speed in the order of 22/23 knots. Her hull form however follows the British rather than the Italian influence and in itself would not be out of place in rough water in, for instance, the English Channel.

One of the most extravagant yachts ever built was commissioned in 1961 for Mr Stavros Niarchos. The motor yacht *Mercury*, 102 feet in length, was powered for a service speed of 50 knots by three Bristol Proteus gas turbines. Almost 40 per cent of her was given up to machinery and tanks, and the owner's accommodation in fact consisted of two guest cabins in addition to his own. Since her auxiliary engines for electricity supply were Rover gas tubines, *Mercury* is very likely the first motor yacht without a piston engine on board. She was a close relation in fact to the *Brave* class patrol boats manufactured by her builders, Vospers of Portsmouth, but magnificently fitted out with, of course, full air conditioning and space heating. Gas turbines, it is reported, have proved a little unpopular when blasting out their hot effluent through mansized holes in the transom in crowded harbours. It may be this aspect of gas turbines or just the sheer cost of an aircraft-type installation which led the 71-foot *Crest Cutter*, originally planned for a triple gas turbine installation, to be redesigned by Cox & Haswell for an eventual triple diesel installation. Although the turbine has a great many attractions for yacht use, small size and smoothness among them, full application to yachts has yet to come.

The big yachts of the Mediterranean are the international yachts, built and manned to standards well above merchant shipping. Whether they are purely private or, as is common, charter yachts they have to be extremely safe and reliable. The cost per day if you are chartering, or the cost per day of the owner's private use taken over the whole season's costing, is such as to make a modest delay through a minor failure a catastrophe. Add to that the sheer capital insurance value of the owner and his guests assessed on their life assurances and so on, and an apparently modest yachting disaster could have financial repercussions as big as a bank failure.

The vast yachts of the Edwardians have passed and in fact the accommodation of a modern small motor yacht, thanks to the diesel engine, is every bit as large. *Aetea*, for instance, a 105-footer designed by Laurent Giles in 1964, is built as a yacht for two families, complete with playroom. Her on-deck accommodation is lavish and runs the full length of the deckhouse with the wheel and chart house on the upper deck. Twin 230-hp Gardner diesels give her a speed of 12 knots. She is designed especially for the hot weather and is extensively air conditioned and, like most yachts of any size, has a large deep freeze capacity, in this case some 30 cubic feet. A yacht of this consequence carries a crew of about six with the captain and the number two, probably the chef, with their own single cabins. The rest of the crew sleep in a forecastle type of compartment but with a separate mess room.

The Italian firm of Benetti are well known for large handsome motor yachts, beautifully furnished. The 25-metre (82-footer) is a semi-production construction yacht with two double guest cabins and an owner's suite. With twin 1,200-hp diesels she has a 20-knot performance. As a type they illustrate the increasing importance of the professional crew in yachting. Although not large she has a separate single cabin for the captain, in addition to two small double cabins, galley and separate mess room for her crew. Luxury yachting needs good eating to set it off and a first rate marine chef can not only command handsome pay but also demand that the galley be set in the best part of the accommodation. The galley in the Benetti 25 is typically up in the deckhouse where it has light and air, and amidships where the motion of the yacht is minimised.

American yachting covers an enormous range and distance and wide extents of differing conditions. It is not possible to categorise American yachts quite so neatly but three distinct trends or influences can be traced. First is the east coast yacht where, from Maine to the Bahamas, yachts of considerable size can cruise in sheltered waters. A few days waiting for settled weather may be required for the occasional open water patches while the intracoastal waterway provides almost highway cruising. Add to that the lakes and rivers, and it is clear why a Mediterranean type of yacht can be found all over America, designed for unrigorous boating. Open-sea yachtsman have been seen looking a bit sideways at such yachts as the traditional Chris Craft, a name almost synonymous with American power yachting. Chris Craft now offer such a wide range of craft that cater for the seaworthy, as well as the more peaceful yachting, that their identification with large, lightly built and somewhat chromium-plated craft is probably now unfair. However, the Chris Craft proper is a superb yacht when taken in its own terms. She is lavishly powered both for propulsion and for the auxiliary engines for electricity and so on, and meticulously planned for installations from air conditioning to full navigational electronics. The accommodation is spacious and takes into account the generally large physical frame of many Americans.

Offshore sports fishing is an American sport which spread, and is spreading still, to other parts of the world. The Gulf Stream is probably the prime fishing area and extremely attractive to the sportsman. The sports fishing yacht in America therefore is an open-sea boat above everything else. As the Gulf Stream is perhaps a hundred miles offshore the running hours between port and the fishing grounds are dead time to be got over as fast as possible. The 'sports fisherman' therefore is also typically a fast powerful vessel with speeds of thirty knots not at all uncommon. As her prime function is fishing, the aft end is devoted to the relevant equipment with its large and elaborate fishing chairs. Next most important is the actual control of the boat during the fight with the fish. The flying bridge with its superb view all round and instant communication between helmsman and fisherman is another now normal part of power yachting which owes its origins to the American sports fisherman. Otherwise the accommodation requirements are simple—a deck saloon to relax in during the passage and small sleeping cabins for resting in and for overnight accommodation between fishing.

The fishing yacht is generally of fairly modest size—say about 40 feet, but the Hatteras company of North Carolina build a range which goes up to 58 feet in length in glass fibre construction and the Rybovich company builds sports fishing yachts whose quality in yacht terms alone is as high as any yacht designed only for more gentle pursuits.

In contrast to the sheltered eastern edge of America, the West Coast faces the full scend of the Pacific all the way from China, with a rocky coast with extremely few harbours of refuge. Add to that a very extensive logging area which lets loose hundreds of semi-submerged tree trunks at the Canadian end to fill the sea with hazards particularly dangerous for fast craft. The West Coast yacht as a type is essentially sturdy and heavily based on local sea-going fishing craft. The type tends to be strongest at the Canadian end while rather more sunshine-oriented craft are often imported for the southern seas of the Los Angeles area.

A typical West Coast craft designed by the Vancouver designer William Garden is *Kakki M*, a 77-footer with 17 feet beam and a fine sweeping sheer. The forward accommodation with three double cabins is below the main deck, but at the aft end of the vessel the deck level drops behind full-height bulwarks so that a protected deck saloon and galley can be arranged on a split level from the forward accommodation. The hull space under the deckhouse contains the tanks and machinery while a pilot house and small funnel sit on top. Twin 326-hp Caterpillar diesels give her a speed of 11 knots and she carries no less than ten tons of fuel.

Another yacht from the same designer is the 94-foot *Hildur* with a range of 3,500 miles at 11 knots. She has the same basic layout as *Kakki M* with a similar beautiful seaworthy double-ended hull. She is intended for Pacific Island cruising and is fitted with a full range of navigational equipment including a fresh water evaporator capable of supplying up to two tons of fresh water every day. Her accommodation consists of three double staterooms each with private bath and shower and the crew accommodation includes separate cabins for cook, engineer and captain.

The islands of the Pacific ocean are becoming increasingly popular as cruising grounds for the larger yachts and this kind of long range and very seaworthy motor yacht is characteristic of the species.

The Enfield-built, Shead-designed *Unowot*, winner of the 1973 Cowes/Torquay/Cowes race.

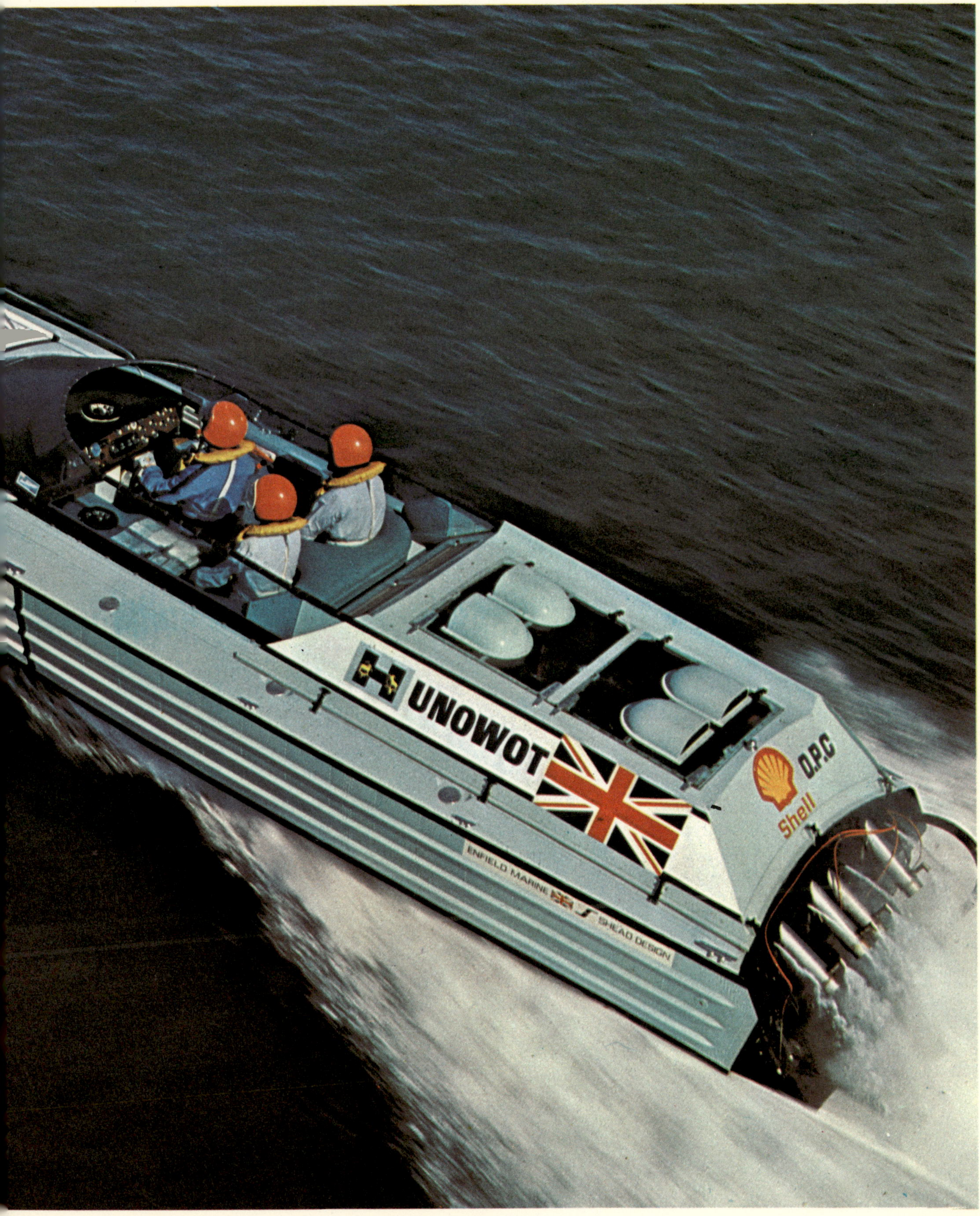
UNOWOT
Shell
D.P.C
ENFIELD MARINE
SHEAD DESIGN

Engines and Installations

There are two main sources of power units for yachts. First is the genuine marine engine designed and built exclusively for use at sea; second is a wide range of engines originally designed for some other industry, usually mass produced and then adapted for the sea. A power unit used for propelling a boat has a quite different pattern of use to, say, a car engine. The latter runs for short periods with continuously varying speed and power output to suit both the driver's foot and the ups and downs and roundabouts of the road. The marine engine in commercial use will normally run at a constant speed near the top of its output for long periods, even up to days at a time. The car engine is designed for a good power output in the middle speed band to give good accelerating characteristics; the commercial boat engine looks for power only at the top end of the range to suit the propeller. The yacht comes somewhere in between the two with much less continuous heavy duty wear but with a distinct interest in top speed. Yacht machinery is under-used compared with most engine applications in terms of engine running hours, but may well be as heavily used in terms of the numbers of start, run, and stop cycles in any year.

The true marine engine is designed round three basic understandings. First is that weight as such is not very important to the slow boats that use them while reliability is. This leads to extra margins of strength being tucked in everywhere and a generally slow running motor to cut stresses. Second is the obvious sense of using the sea all around the boat for cooling. To avoid the salt evaporating and caking inside the engine, larger cooling galleries are required compared with fresh water, again increasing the sheer bulk of the engine. The third factor is the unsophisticated approach to maintenance which might be expected from the crews of small commercial craft. Again this leads to extra margins of strength all round together with an avoidance of any sophisticated design or equipment which might otherwise have pumped up the performance.

The slow yacht, in the past, usually plumped for the true marine engine for the same reasons of reliability and so on as the commercial craft. Some current construction in fact still employs them but this is probably more of an indication of a conservative industry than a true implication of their being more suitable for yachts than the rest. The marine based engine cannot compete for costing with the full production line unit. It is heavy where most yachts are looking for lighter weights and improved performance and it is bulky, thereby biting into the accommodation payload. Reliability then remains as the only area of competition but this is now increasingly

The original single Parsons radial flow turbine of *Turbinia* which was later replaced with three parallel flow turbines connected in series.

A Daimler marine engine of 1898.

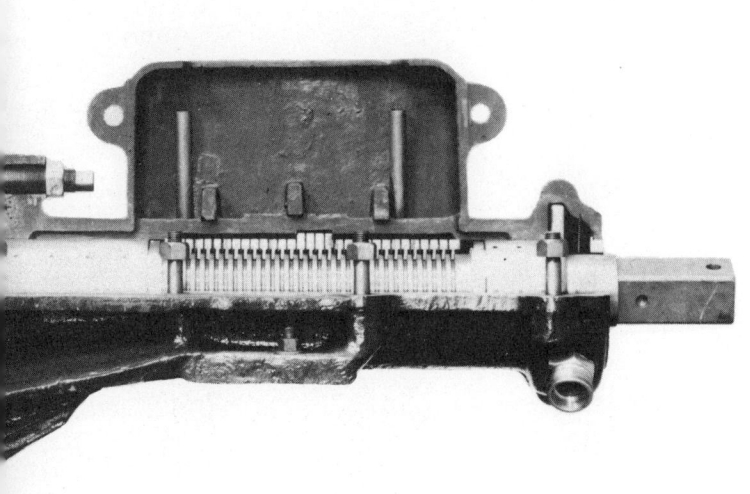

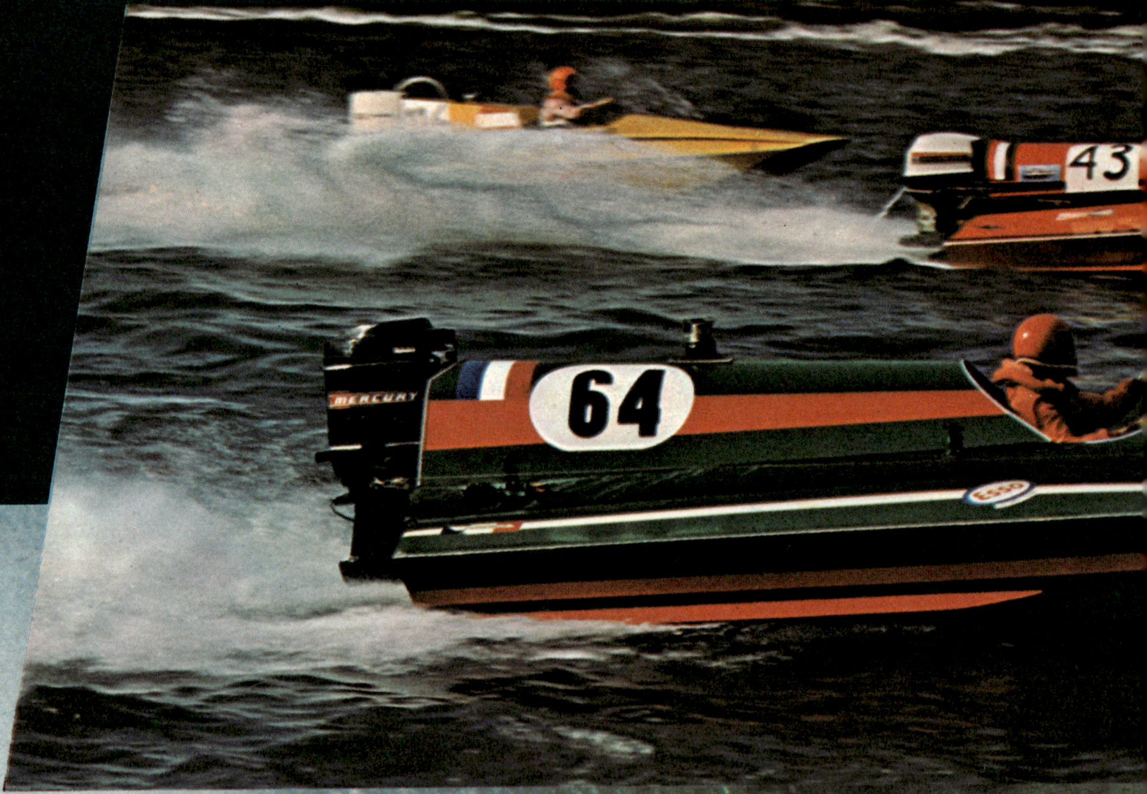
43
64
MERCURY

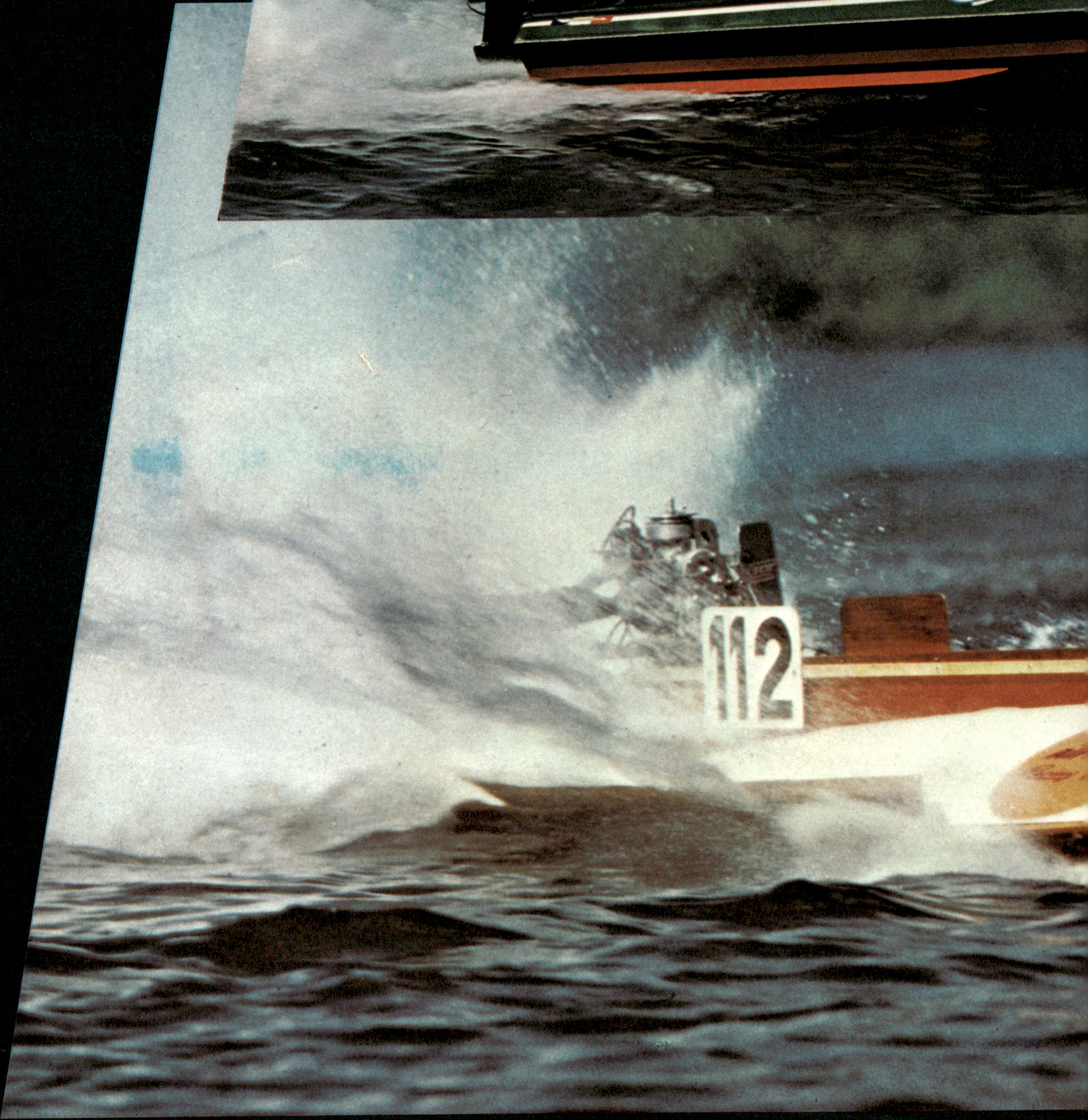
112

left: The Paris Six Hour race is one of the circuit racing classics for small powerboats.

below: The true skimming dish, hydroplane racing is a fast and specialised sport on its own.

The propeller and rudder arrangement of *Miss England II* is strikingly similar to the modern "zip strut" but contrasts with the cooling pipes and nuts and bolts above it.

The De Havilland Ghost jet engine used by John Cobb in his *Crusader* was capable of delivering a thrust of 5,000 lb.

The control panel of *Crusader*.

thought to be almost synonymous with servicing and here the multiple production engines can score heavily with trained agents and depots all over the world.

Petrol engines are light, quiet and inexpensive and use expensive fuel. Diesel engines are heavy, noisy, smelly, expensive, and use inexpensive fuel. On this basis the choice of engine is almost one of the economics of first cost against running costs, modified by the extra costs of reducing noise and smell to acceptable limits. Petrol, however, vaporises readily and especially in hot climates into an explosive mixture and is generally considered as being undesirable for yachts of any size. In fact, in the Mediterranean it is so badly considered that yachts are reluctant to moor alongside a petrol-powered craft. This poor reputation for petrol fuel is not really justified except in relation to poor installations and bad maintenance. Witness, for instance, the almost universal use of petrol powered cars and planes in the same geographical areas. It is true, however, that the penalties for misuse are both immediate and explosive. Diesel with its higher flashpoint is considered as safe and the smell tends to be accepted as normal. The paraffin-powered engine is really an economic variation of the petrol spark-ignited unit and has now largely disappeared except for quite small craft.

With the worldwide use of diesel engines for farm and earth moving equipment and so on, and also for trucks and even tanks, there has grown up a wide range of high output commercial diesel engines and it is these, in their marine conversions, that power most yachts these days. Conversion from the assembly line involves primarily a check on all the materials used and replacement where necessary with parts which can stand up to the corrosive sea air and the occasional salt spray coming in through the vents. A closed circuit cooling system has to be fitted to retain the use of fresh water in the engine but a heat exchanger and an additional circulating pump have to be added to allow salt water cooling of the fresh water. A marine gearbox has to be added, probably with an integral reduction box, and the main sump will probably have to be redesigned to suit the changed angle of installation normal for marine use. Components may have to be relocated so that they remain accessible in engine room maintenance, and last but not least, the fuel pumps and injector characteristics may have to be changed to suit a different power output curve and a different exhaust back pressure range. Most engine makers are on a power output rating race against weight at the moment, and engine revolution speeds and compression ratios have been getting higher and higher. In turn this has meant more noise and greater stress but in most cases, if the engines are considered at cruising rather than sprint conditions, they are getting quieter and more reliable.

Although there are such animals as diesel-engined raceboats they are so handicapped by the weight of their engines that they compete for special category prizes only. The top speed raceboats until the full introduction of gas turbines are entirely equipped with petrol engines. The offshore power boat racing rules were in fact drawn up for the biggest flat-out class around the availability of American car and truck petrol engines of about eight litres. A maximum capacity allowance of just over sixteen litres allows two such units to be fitted, giving, after marinising and tuning, a total power of between 800 and 1,000 hp. These engine limits are both sensible and a very great pity. They are sensible because when they were introduced the cheapest engines on a power/cost basis were these units produced by Detroit in tens of thousands. In fact basically the situation still applies today, but the cost of highly tuned engines which may now only be rated for a ten-hour racing life has spiralled to prohibitive levels. At the same time the rule has swamped any engine production initiative anywhere else in the world. A similar picture can be seen arising out of the prospective gas turbine rules.

Raceboat engines and installations really have a very hard life, in fact it is difficult to think of any other device that offers an engine a worse working environment particularly in terms of movement. A raceboat in rough water being driven with enthusiasm takes a pounding which no other vehicle known to man puts up with. The craft bounces off the sea to crash back with accelerometer readings of 8g or 9g fairly common and figures in the 20g range not unknown. This means that at 9g every part suddenly becomes the equivalent of ten times heavier for an instant and compares with the figures of less than 1g recommended for public transport and the 5g limits of military aircraft. A mine going off is reckoned to give shocks of 30g in a single near miss but the hard riding power boat is taking not dissimilar shocks every few seconds. In a single race the hull and machinery may have to withstand as many as 3,000 such shocks.

The really important thing about a raceboat installation is that it shall last the race, for without finishing there is no winning. The quality of the installation is therefore judged in terms of say four hours of complete reliability. Special gadgets and engineering tricks which improve performance on paper are judged on the same reliability basis and more often than not the verdict is on the side of simplicity. The installation is therefore above all simple and solid with every possible pipe, wire and connection strapped down to hard structure to stop it waving and wearing or ageing when the craft is in motion. In addition, the ordinary installation components, switches, valves, and so on, may have to be specially built to take the shock loading since there is no ready supply from any other industry to be tapped.

The classic inboard-engined raceboat will therefore have a very simple installation with twin engines bolted solidly through reinforced feet to heavy bearers and connected direct to twin shafts without intermediate shafts or flexible couplings. A possible acceptable complication is to couple both engines to a single twin input/single output gearbox to achieve the simplification and reduced drag of a single propeller. Most boats still work with a straight drive, or more accurately 1:1 ratio gear box but the surface propeller is coming back again into fashion and this may involve using a gear box which actually increases the propeller rpm to say 10,000 rpm compared with the 6,000 of the engine crankshaft.

left: The offshore racing catamaran *Black Panther.*

below: The 29-foot offshore racing catamaran *Miss Guernsey*, designed by James Beard and built by Cougar Marine.

The other problem in flying and bouncing as far as the engine is concerned is that of bouncing the propeller clean out of the water when the engine, suddenly running light, starts to race only to be brought up short again when the propeller dips in. Apart from the possible damage this might cause to the engine the interruption in actual propeller propulsion is a dead loss as far as performance goes. The actual flying on the other hand if properly controlled is sheer bonus in reduced skin friction. The raceboat ideal therefore is to fly the hull as much as possible while keeping the propeller working. One answer is to extend the shaft aft down beyond the transom supported by a strut aft of the propeller, known as the zip strut if it also carries the rudder. This has the effect of reducing the apparent rise of the boat which is usually bow first and delaying the onset of propeller race. A certain degree of semi-surface propellers are used, but in a rough water boat it is difficult to be certain about the conditions in which a full surface propeller will find itself during most of the race.

The limiting equipment in current raceboat design is still probably her human crew. It is possible, given the costs, to engineer the hull and machinery to withstand even more punishment in rough water and even to improve the flying characteristics of the hull. However, the rules require the raceboats to have human drivers and navigators and these have to be very carefully packaged and installed. The average raceboat cockpit is therefore something of an upholstery mine designed on the best ergonomic principles to reduce suffering. Essentially the pelvis has to be quite well restrained from movement with the body north and south of it progressively allowed more movement to give some muscular springing of the human hard structure. The vibration and jarring make accurate readings of instruments difficult and therefore these are enlarged and simplified. The compass, for instance, is heavily damped, all navigation worked out before the race, and courses painted on the deck in large letters. Driving and control techniques vary a great deal with both the style and skill of the driver. Basically some like to leave the engine speed controls alone and use heavy steering to find a way through the wave pattern. Others like to make continual variations to speed to suit the instantaneous wave situation and these latter will probably make use of a foot throttle pedal while the former use the more conventional lever control. Gear levers are regarded as secondary controls as they are normally only used before the start or after the finish and they can therefore be situated less conveniently to the hand than in a cruising boat. The prime function of the steering is after all to direct the course of the boat but the first action of a rudder in a high-speed boat, particularly if of deep vee form, is to bank the hull in the direction in which the top of the wheel is moved. This is an invaluable control facility as it allows the driver some choice of the hull attitude to meet each sea. It is often softer to land the boat on her

The Kelvin TASC6 diesel engine is turbo-charged and intercooled and is designed primarily for marine propulsion.

Gar Wood at the controls of *Miss America X* showing her quadruple Packard engines.

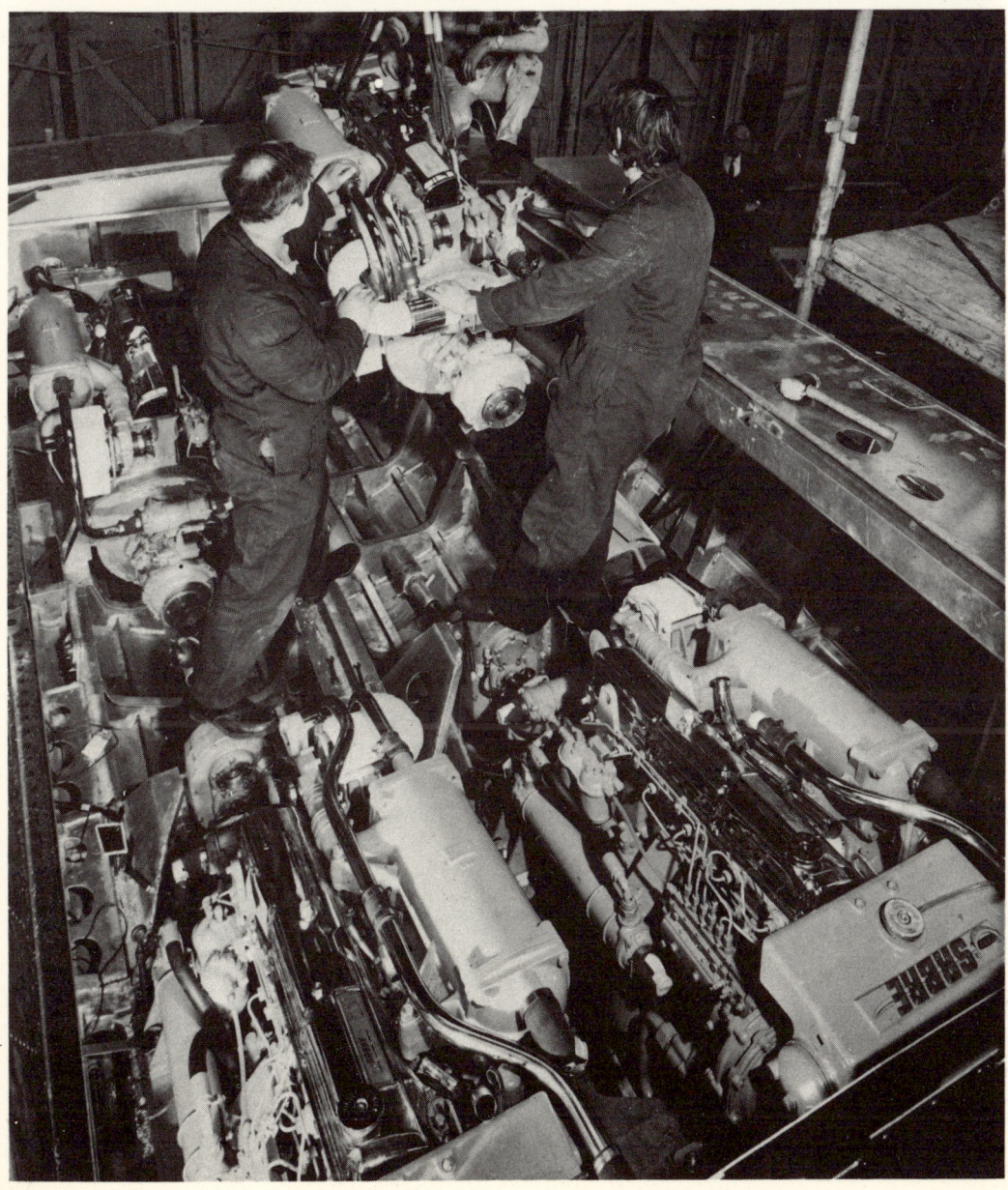

A quadruple installation of Ford Sabre diesels.

49

At speed in the Paris Six Hour race.

Peter Thorneywork winning the outboard ON class at Milan 1974.

right: The engine room of a Grand Banks 48, fitted with twin 6 cylinder Ford diesels. The generator in its sound box can be seen behind the engineer.

below: The control room of the gas turbine yacht *Mercury*.

chine rather than flat on her full bottom.

Nearly every race boat is fitted with trim tabs. These are flap type extensions to the aft planing surface and are adjustable as to angle by a cockpit control. A trim tab when lying in line with the planing bottom or a degree or two up from it has no effect on the basic running trim of the hull. If, however, it is trimmed down so as to form a drooping flap it will have a considerable effect in dropping the bow and reducing the hull angle of attack. The preferred hull trim varies with different sea conditions and the pilot can therefore use his trim tabs to adjust to conditions as he meets them along the course. In addition, however, he can also use them independently to iron out such things as propeller torque or unequal fuel tank weights. In flat water a fairly high bow up trim is generally best in reducing to a minimum the skin friction but in rougher water a much lower trim is desirable both for the extra waterline length and for the reduction in actual bow movement when bounced on a sea.

Some boats, though very few these days, are fitted with ballast tanks for the same job. The driver can open a cock which allows sea water to be scooped into a tank generally fitted fairly well forward with the object of both increasing the weight of the boat in general and reducing the trim in particular. At the onset of calmer conditions the tank can be emptied again by another valve. The use of ballast in rough water is not easily justified technically but stems from a quite deep-rooted opinion among seamen that the heavier boat is the better boat in rough water.

The only real feature which the cruising power yacht shares with the raceboat is that ever-present marine need for reliability. The cruising yacht sets a number of secondary targets quite high and these include quietness, safety, freedom from odours, and ease of maintenance, all inside the pressures of accommodation space. The logical position for the engines, just about amidships with simple straight forward shafting, is unfortunately bang in the best accommodation space in the yacht. An engine room amidships with its water and oil tight bulkheads effectively divides the accommodation into two. It is therefore not uncommon to find the shaft angles reversed with a vee drive allowing the engines to be arranged right aft and the hull accommodation to be uninterrupted. The weight distribution of this arrangement is not ideal but is increasingly more practical as engines get lighter. The vee drives are either quite separate units or are sometimes incorporated in the main engine gearbox.

Quietness in an installation starts with the reduction of transmitted noise and vibration. Flexible mountings are often used in cars to dampen out engine vibrations and these are quite common in yacht installations. However they require some elaboration of the installation to take account of the increased physical movement of the engine itself. This means that pipe connections have to have final flexible sections at the engine. Fuel and water are not too difficult to arrange but big exhaust pipes are more difficult. The connections to the shaft can be cumbersome and involve twin flexible couplings with intermediate shaft to cater for the parallel axis of the moving engine and fixed shaft line. It is also more than likely that a thrust block would be required to take the propeller thrust off the whole assembly. The shaft itself leaves the hull through a gland and tube which is usually water cooled with a bleed from the main engine water cooling system. This not only cools the gland but allows water lubricated rubber bearings to be fitted as standard both in the shaft tube and in the one or two shaft bearing brackets required to support the shaft outside the hull.

In the days of physically large engines it was not always possible to place the fuel tanks near the engine and sometimes difficult to ensure that the fuel lift pump would always be effective. In that situation it was normal to fit a header tank supplying fuel direct to the engine. This was pumped up at regular intervals either by a mechanical pump but often by the ship's engineer applying himself to a hand pump. Nowadays fuel systems which draw direct from the tanks are very common especially when the tanks are in the engine space. The concentration of all the smells and fuel drips in a separated and well ventilated compartment is very desirable and insulation and fuel coolers can be fitted to prevent the fuel warming up.

The other component of combustion, air, is required in considerable quantities by a high revving engine with, say, a 16:1 compression ratio. Large vent areas are necessary, aided by mechanical fans. If the engine room is open to the main accommodation an extractor fan may be fitted with an induced supply both to the engine and to ventilate the engine space proper. The slight reduction in engine room air pressure sucks air in from the surrounding accommodation instead of releasing engine room smells to it. In a hot climate, however, the extractor fan will be whirling fairly uselessly in the superhot engine room air and it is necessary to put all the fans at the other end of the system drawing in the cooler ambient air to push out the hot.

Engine cooling ultimately is effected by the sea. Most commonly salt water is admitted through a seacock and strainer and circulated through a heat exchanger mounted on the engine to cool the fresh water circulating around the engine itself. The warm sea water is then usually injected into the exhaust system or pumped overboard with a portion taken to the stern tubes. In steel yachts the system is often simplified to use the skin of the yacht itself as the heat exchanger. The hot fresh water is pumped from the engine through a shallow compartment welded direct to the skin of the yacht. Another variation of this takes the fresh water pipes through the hull on a closed circuit tour of the cool water outside for so-called keel cooling.

The exhaust can be disposed of in three separate directions, each with some disadvantage. The most common solution numerically perhaps is to lift a dry exhaust pipe as high as possible, inject water into it and run the combined exhaust and water downhill and away to the shipside or all the way to the transom via a silencer. The water injection cools the hot gases and the consequent shrinkage in volume reduces the back pressure and upsets the noise patterns to achieve some silencing. A side exhaust can be tiresome in letting fumes

54

left: The Levi-designed *Hydrosonic Special* built in 1967, showing both the power of the modern raceboat and the porpoising action used to reduce skin friction.

below left: The Riva *Super Aquarama*, a 28-ft 10-in fast power boat.
below: Thunderfish in rough water.

come back on board especially when they are reflected off the next yacht alongside. A stern exhaust tends to suck back on board when running and the pipes and silencers usually have to be run through the best of the accommodation. The second solution is to fit a dry exhaust and take it straight up through a silencer to discharge through a funnel. This requires quite high funnels to ensure that the effluent is carried well clear of the white flannel party on the after deck. Last but not least is to discharge the exhaust, water cooled and all, through the bottom of the yacht. Back pressure can be catered for with a relief pipe to atmosphere and the principal problem is the question of where the discharged gas actually gets to. If it is swept aft in to the propellers it can upset their performance badly and another hazard, not unknown, is for the exhaust to percolate back up through lavatory discharges if these happen to be on its route. Under water exhaust is also supposed to disturb passing fish and therefore should not be used for sports fishing yachts.

Electrics used to have a very bad reputation afloat. There used to be a slightly bitter saying among yachtsmen that the electrical installation was done by the yard labourer when he was not painting the topsides. A lot of things have changed and topsides now invariably sport a sparkling gloss and electrical installations have become well designed and competent. The basis of any electrics in a power yacht is the ability to start the main engines. Like car engines, each yacht engine has its own alternator, supplying, with a bit in hand, 12 or 24-volt DC batteries sufficient to start themselves. The battery capacity is usually increased to run the domestic lighting and navigation lights of the yacht for, say, one full night's load unsupported. This capacity is doubled and separated into two banks so that the engine starting batteries are not affected if the domestic bank should run flat. The additional capacity is charged by auxiliary generators. This can either mean another large capacity alternator run off the main engine power take-off, or, more commonly, a separate single or pair of auxiliary generating engines.

With so much domestic equipment available on 110 or 240 volt AC, cookers, vacuum cleaners, galley mixers, TV, and shavers, to mention but a few, the auxiliary generator set is usually arranged to provide power for this equipment direct, while fitted with a converter which also charges the batteries when the AC circuits are running. Automatic generator engine starting is often used so that the auxiliary engine is only run when an AC appliance is actually switched on. Apart from allowing the extensive use of normal household equipment this system can also easily be plugged into shore supplies when the yacht is in harbour, thereby keeping the whole electrical system in top line without the generating machinery running.

A basic household comfort which is accepted more or less without comment ashore is running hot and cold water. This is accomplished afloat either by use of a header tank with a daily or automatic pump-up schedule or in smaller yachts by a pressure switched on-demand electric pump. A low pressure, a few pounds, is maintained in the piping system. When a tap is turned on the pressure drops and the pressure switch starts the electric pump which continues operating until the tap

left: The inboard/outboard unit makes a convenient installation for many small craft.

right: The simplicity of an outboard engine installation for small boats is shown in this raceboat with its 50-hp Mercury.

below: This marinised automotive petrol engine delivers about 400 hp for its 1000 lb of weight. It is the Daytona Turbo 400 used in many racing powerboats.

is closed and the pressure builds up again to switch-off point. Hot water is heated in normal household gas or electric geysers or immersion-heater type boilers. Oil-burning water heaters are also available and some yachts also take advantage, by means of waste heat boilers fitted around the exhaust pipes, of engine heat that otherwise would be wasted. Lavatory systems vary from pressure flush as fitted in big ships to modest hand-pump-operated units with directly coupled inlet and outlets to the sea. With pollution control gaining strength everywhere the direct discharge of sewage is forbidden in a great many harbours. This is therefore collected in a holding tank on board for sucking out by the harbour authorities or for pumping out when the yacht is at sea. Many yachts, particularly older ones, do not have room for a special holding tank and the associated equipment to meet the new regulations and several ranges of lavatories have been developed where a chemical treatment holding tank is incorporated with the toilet unit. This can be carried bodily ashore for emptying by hand or pumped away at sea.

A yacht, compared with even a modest house, is small in volume for the number of people and the amount of equipment in her. She may also be built of metal, float in a coolish sea in hot sunshine, and live in a corrosive atmosphere. Proper ventilation to equipment and structure is essential to the well-being of the yacht, never mind the owner and his guests. Air conditioning is even better, of course, and it is rare for a yacht of any consequence and meant for the Mediterranean-type of living not to be so fitted. The simplest arrangement consists of individual cabin units just plugged and plumbed into the ship's systems. A central plant in the engine room is more efficient and the refrigerating unit can also be used to run a deep freeze or cold room. Heat for the warming end of air conditioning is often obtained by a small electric element located just behind the outlet grill.

Navigation electronics especially designed for small craft is a thriving industry and it is rare for a yacht to be seen without a fairly comprehensive selection. Top in popularity is a depth sounder, closely followed by a speedometer log. These two, together with the compass, form the basic dead reckoning navigation equipment of any small vessel. Next comes the equipment for radio navigation with a small receiver coupled to a directionally sensitive aerial to pick up the radio beacons specially situated for the mariner. Radar is an invaluable aid to any seafarer and larger yachts quite often also carry automatic navigation systems equipment such as a Loran and a Decca Navigator. Communications radio usually completes the list, with a VHF set for local use and a single side band radio/telephone for long range. Single side band sets are now mandatory on the medium frequency bands and can be arranged for duplex working if required to give telephone-type talking. The range of electronics is probably completed with an automatic pilot, an almost universal fitment on all but the smaller yachts. Hand steering, except in and out of harbour, is quite rare. The control station of the average power vessel nowadays has a closer resemblance to a space craft than to any old fashioned picture of oilskin clad figures wrestling with a large teak-spoked brass-bound wheel in the midst of the windy worst of the elements.

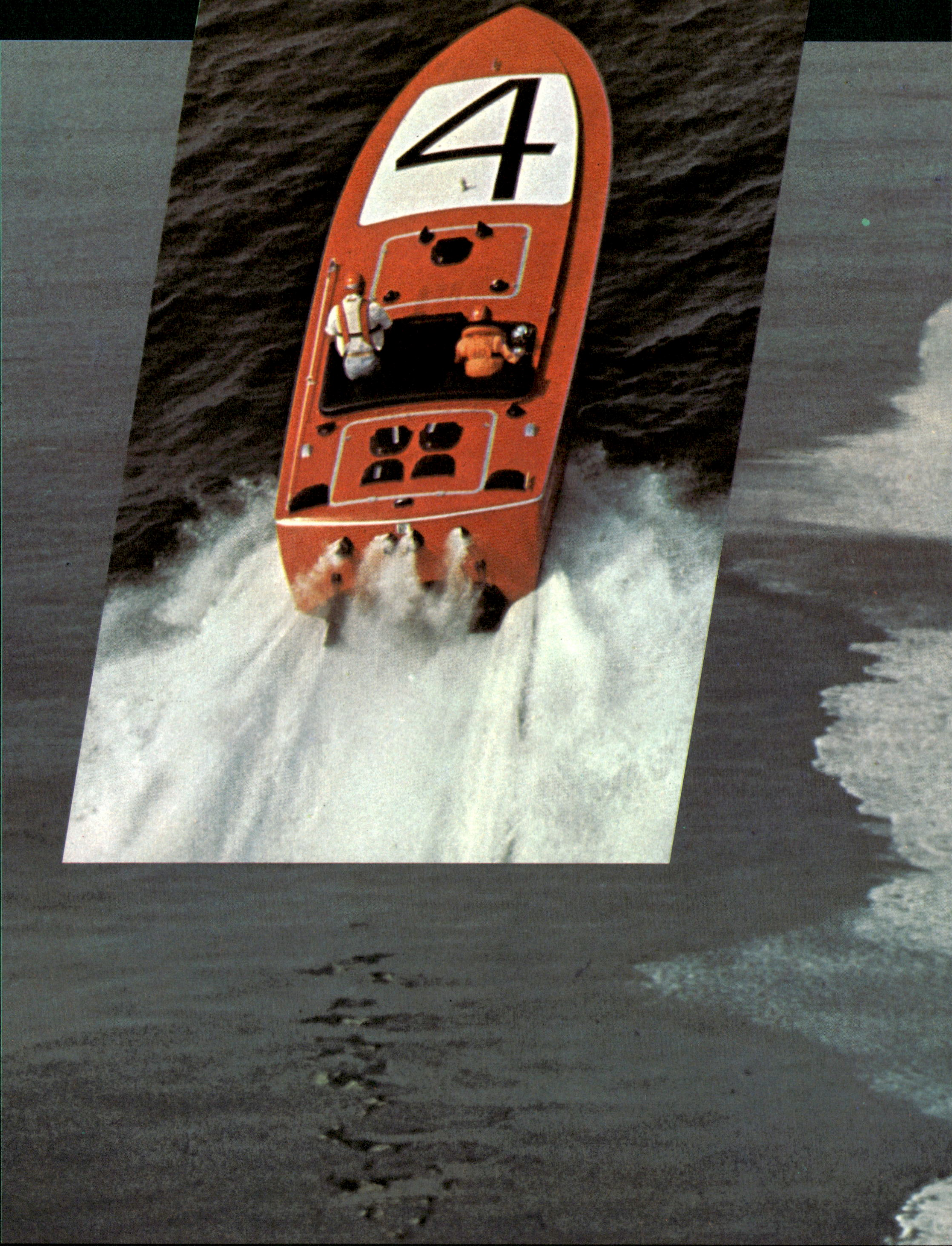
4

Red Tornado, a 31-foot Bertram, raced by the Italian driver, Balestrieri, in 1969.

Modern Power Boat Racing

Jim Wynne won the 1966 Daily Express Offshore Power Boat Race in the 28 ft *Ghostrider*. His engineer, Bob Sherbert had both ankles broken.

For nearly fifty years the British International Trophy, formerly the Harmsworth Trophy, was the top goal for power boat racers. For thirty nine of those years it was held exclusively by the Americans but in 1959 this long run was broken by the Canadian boat *Miss Supertest III* at Detroit. In the following year she won again with a speed of 116 mph, the top speed over the whole range of the contests. In the next year, 1961, she won again at a very much reduced speed and that was that. After three years without contest the series lapsed and the trophy returned to the keeping of the Royal Motor Yacht Club at Poole. There have been various thoughts on reviving or re-allocating this trophy, as famous and as fought over in its time as the America's Cup, but the contest is unlikely to come back in its original form. Three races around a forty mile course in unlimited-power forty-footers have been completely superseded in public interest by the same size of craft with limited power competing on offshore touring courses up to more than 200 miles in length. Fast power boat men are of course as competitive and proud of their craft as anyone else afloat and two or three craft proceeding together at any time are usually engaged in some kind of contest, albeit unofficial. Formal offshore racing started, or perhaps re-started, when Red Crise and Sam Griffith, both Miamians, rounded up some thirty boats in 1956 for an all-out race from Miami to Nassau. This was during a period when the fast offshore power boat was generally developing as a boat type in its own right on the back of post-war engine production. Sir Max Aitken, himself a fast power boat enthusiast, saw the possibilities for improving the breed through competition much in the way that motor racing is used in the car industry. In 1961 he originated the Cowes/Torquay race for cruising power boats.

The problems and responsibilities of starting an open water race for craft which hitherto went to sea with circumspection were heavy. The first Cowes/Torquay race was organised with enormous care and in fact set a standard which is still evident all through power boat racing. First, the entries were grouped by size and engine power and each group was required to have a certain degree of accommodation and furnishings. On deck there was a limit on the size of open cockpits and specific requirements on the seamanship and rescue fittings and equipment. All this was checked thoroughly the day before the race by a team of scrutineers and all boats had to be up to scratch

inset: The Levi-designed *Surfury* had a long and successful career in the hands of the Gardner brothers.

inset: Tramontana II first raced in 1963 fitted with four Jaguar car engines.

A raceboat at speed.

before they were allowed even to start the race. Drivers and crews were formally briefed on weather reports, racing rules, hazards along the course, and the rescue arrangements. Even the start was kept firmly under control. A big group of power boats only semi-controllable at semi-planing speeds frothing along among their own washes cannot be allowed to spin and manoeuvre for the best positions as at the start of a sailing yacht race. The rolling start was devised with everyone lining up beside a starting vessel. She moved off at a speed of fifteen knots towards the actual starting line with the fleet in line abreast beside her. Not until the starting gun fired were the race boats allowed to open wide and accelerate off. Not only does this arrangement give a first rate start with time for everyone to get exactly in line with each other but it ensures that the race actually starts at planing speeds where race boats are really under better control.

The Royal Motor Yacht Club, the Royal Torbay Yacht Club, the Royal Yacht Squadron, together with the Royal Navy and the Royal Air Force Sea Rescue were enrolled to help. The government boats provided the starting ship and patrol craft which followed the racers along the course. The yacht clubs provided liaison, mark boats, and local patrol and rescue boats along the way. In addition, to promote public interest in an event which is spectacular but strung out, loudspeaker commentaries were arranged at the best vantage points for spectators.

This first race was undoubtedly a slog. The day was windy and overcast and the sea in Lyme Bay was rough. In fact many of the true cruising boats assembled at the start would not normally have put to sea in such conditions. Many competitors also completely underestimated the amount of fuel which would be used in bucking into a big head sea and mechanical and structural problems were common. Out of twenty-eight starters in fact only nine boats actually finished, leaving coasts and harbours along the course fairly strewn with sea-damaged craft. The top favourite for the race was the 31-foot *Glass Moppie* with 660 hp, late winner of the Miami/Nassau race and driven by Sam Griffith himself. However, after leading the fleet she dropped out with gearbox trouble and the race for a while developed into a contest between Renato Levi in the 26-foot *A'Speranziella* with 600 hp, Tommy Sopwith's 25-foot 650-hp *Thunderbolt* and Jim Wynne's 21-foot, 200-hp *Yo Yo*. The eventual winner was *Thunderbolt* at a time of 7 hours 20 minutes for the 156 nautical mile course, a speed of just under 22 knots or 25 mph. *Yo Yo*, the very much smaller boat was in fact less than half an hour behind. No outboard-powered boats finished the course even though one stopped to buy more fuel from a Russian tanker on the way. It is also

right: A'Speranziella, winner of the 1963 Cowes/Torquay race, designed and driven by Sonny Levi and the forerunner of a very successful series.

far right: Sam Griffith and Dick Bertram racing the Hunt designed *Blue Moppie*.

worth noting that five of the nine boats which finished the race were to the deep vee design of American Ray Hunt, which became the parent classic hull form for a great many rough water cruising fast boats.

Despite a first race which produced results which looked very little advanced compared with, say, 1904 when the Harmsworth Trophy and the Cross Channel race were run at comparable speeds and with a greater proportion of finishers, offshore power boating was back in Britain, again, to stay. The Cowes/Torquay became a yearly event and the principal and classic event of a revived sport.

The following year there were forty-two starters for the second race with Sam Griffith and Dick Bertram entered with a new boat, *Blue Moppie*, powered by 660 hp. However, in memory perhaps of the Gar Wood approach to speed Dick Wilkins had asked Vospers to put a hull round two enormous Isotta Fraschini engines adding up to no less than 2,308 hp. *Tramontana*, as she was called, duly won the race with *Blue Moppie* second. This race also had its share of casualties, one boat sank and another turned turtle.

The year 1963 brought the introduction of new engine capacity rules based on the American raceboats, effectively ruling the mighty *Tramontana* out of racing altogether. Dick Wilkins very sportingly built a new *Tramontana* with four Jaguar car engines which finished third, although she had to retire for a course error. The winner was Renato Levi in *A'Speranziella* but the notoriety in this race went to Dr Savundra whose *Jackie S* pursued an erratic course which included ramming the Needles' light rounding up to a collision under the bows of another boat and running over and sinking a harmless spectator craft.

The following year was a flat-water fast contest with the winners, Charles and Jimmy Gardner, putting up an average speed of 49 mph in *Surfrider*. Dick Bertram in *Lucky Moppie* actually arrived first at the finish but missed winning because of a navigational error at the line. In 1965 however he made sure that there would be no mistakes and embarked Michael Richey, Britain's premier small boat navigator and executive secretary of the Royal Institute of Navigation, and won the race in the 31-foot Hunt-designed *Brave Moppie* with 1,100 hp of diesel engines. This was also the first race for the famous *Surfury* designed by Levi for the Gardner brothers, who after some mechanical troubles with a new boat came in third. *Surfury* was an offshore development of a Levi design which had proved itself in smaller sizes. Two Daytona engines of 1,000 hp total were coupled to a single shaft to give her a speed up in the 70 mph range, but her long fine deeply veed hull shape was really the first pointer to the real shape for offshore race boats.

Only slightly modified from a standard runabout, the Riva *Zoom* achieved second place in the Monte Carlo marathon powerboat race, at nearly 5,000 miles the longest ever run.

inset: Avenger Too, driven by Timo Makinen to win the 1969 Round Britain powerboat race.

right: There have been few more consistent finishers than the beautiful, diesel powered, *Gipsy Girl,* designed by Hunt for Sir Max Aitken.

below right: Uffa Fox standing beside his stepped hydroplane, *Black Maria,* which he designed for Sir Max Aitken.

By this time the accommodation rules for the flat-out boats had become anachronistic. The actual rule furniture and fittings were pared to the irreducible to save weight and the rule upholstery and crockery carried on board only for scrutineering and the race. The cabin volume requirements were covered with bulging deckworks and visiting American flat out boats had to rebuild their decks to suit. Plainly it was time to extend the rules to a new class which was designated, curiously, OP, standing for Open Pleasure, and to set up a scheme of world wide regulations. To maintain the original objective of improving cruising boats, however, the cruiser classes were not only maintained but encouraged with the major share of the prize money. The OP-type classes however have won every race outright since they were allowed into the Cowes/Torquay, although the cabin boats have at times run them surprisingly close.

The sixth race in 1966 was won by Jim Wynne driving a boat of his own design, *Ghost Rider,* built at Cowes by the now famous race boat builders of W A Souter & Son. She covered the 172 nautical miles at an average speed of 41 mph. Rough water in Lyme Bay sorted out the fleet of fifty starters and a surprisingly small number, eighteen, actually finished. *Ghost Rider* was only 28 feet in length, powered by twin Daytonas giving 1,000 hp but the second boat home was a real cruising boat, *Spirit of Ecstasy,* with only 920 hp of Rolls-Royce diesel to drive her 42 feet. The following year, 1967, was the first flat-water race along that course and this really showed up the reliability of boats pushed to their top speeds for anything up to six hours or so. Of seventy starters only thirty nine finished the course, leaving one to burn out and sink and another to catch alight although extinguished. The beautiful *Surfury* finished the race first in 3 hours 44 minutes at an average speed of 53 mph with the Italian *Delta Synthesis,* also a Levi design, second. The much larger number in this race is accounted for by the race committee allowing for the first time entries from craft down to 20 feet in length.

By contrast 1968 was a really tough race and run on a longer and harder course. Instead of the finishing line being at Torquay itself the race was extended to return to Cowes, increasing the length to 230 miles. This course change was not only an extension of the toughness of the race itself but some answer to criticism that it was a largely one way test into the prevailing south westerly winds and took very little account of the ability of fast boats to travel safely in the opposite direction. In many ways running downwind is much more difficult for a power boat than banging into wind and sea. The surface drift and wave movement help her along but may accelerate her at the wrong moment to drive into the wave face or to pick up her stern and swing her into an uncontrolled broach. The year 1968 set up real conditions for such trials with the strongest winds ever and a 75-mile real open water run first into and then with the weather. The big boats like *Surfury* appeared to forge ahead but skill and tactics won the day for Tommy Sopwith in his tiny Don Shead designed *Telstar,* a 25-footer powered by a single Daytona Scarab engine with 600 hp. While the open water in Lyme Bay slowed down the leaders and sank *Magnum Tornado*, little *Telstar* took the long course round the edge of the land with easier seas and much more shelter. In fact, out of sight and rather out of mind, her prowess was not reported and *Surfury*, confident of winning, took life on the easy side on the way back, only to find little *Telstar* tucked into the winner's berth at Cowes. At the same time the race showed that the modern racing power boat with its deep vee and needle nose could cope very well with heavy following sea conditions.

A flat calm contrasted the following year and Don Aronow, the American World Champion, set up a record for the course of no less than 66 mph with his 1,000-hp *Cigarette* to his own design. In shape she was a compromise form between the deep vee darts of the Europeans and the wide-bowed constant-section Hunt American type. With 32 feet of slim hull she was the first winner of this race to be fitted with outdrive units. Another interesting and significant boat which appeared for this race was the welded aluminium Shead-designed *Miss Enfield* with two Mercruiser engines giving 950 hp and illustrating a trend away from the moulded wood boats.

Her successor, *Miss Enfield II* by the same designer, won the race for the third time for Tommy Sopwith in 1970 in a race which touched 70 mph in the sheltered areas in a close competition with the Italians Balestrieri and Cosentino. In 1971 there was another really rough-

69

Enfield Avenger, designed by Don Shead for aluminium construction.

The classic raceboats of the seventies, the Cigarette series show the slim lines of the type.

water race where even the World Champion Bill Wishnick in a 32-foot *Cigarette*-type raceboat called *Boss O'Nova II* underestimated the fuel required to bash into big seas and had to return while leading the race into Lyme Bay. The winner was a Don Aronow design, *Lady Nara,* driven by Ronnie Bonelli. Some 60 miles from the finish she hit a large sea, pitching both Bonelli and a mechanic from the cockpit onto the engine cowling and knocking them semi-conscious. Commander Petroni, the co-driver, completed the course and *Lady Nara's* winning time averaged 38 mph. It was a race which took a heavy toll and of the forty-one actual starters only twelve completed the 245-mile course and two of those came in after the ten and a half hour time limit. The 1972 race was another which promised to be rough but with the winds in the north east the seas did not build up as in other times. The first two boats home were Italian owned *Cigarette*-types with *Aeromarine IX* driven by Carlo Bonomi first and *Black Tornado* driven by Balestrieri second, both boats averaging about 55 mph. The 1973 race was dominated again by *Cigarettes* but the actual winner was *Unowot* driven by her designer Don Shead, an aluminium boat built by Enfield in 1971 and re-engined for this race with twin 600-hp Kiekhaefer Aeromarine engines. Second home, only two minutes behind, powered by identical engines, came Giorgio Mondadori in *Nicopao,* a 36-foot *Cigarette*. Third until very close to the finish came yet another *Cigarette* with the same engines, *Dry Martini,* driven by Carlo Bonomi. She had had steering trouble and this finally failed only three hundred yards from the line. While she struggled to finish in great looping uncontrolled circles she was passed by *HTS* which shot in to take the third prize. Gas turbine boats were entered in the race for the first time as an experimental class. Only one actually got to the starting line, *Miss Embassy,* built by Vospers to a Shead design and driven by Tommy Sopwith. This 42-footer with its large and distinctive air intakes was fitted with a single Rolls-Royce Gnome of 1,000 horsepower but proved little competition for the fast boats and eventually retired into Weymouth with mechanical problems. Gas turbines become officially acceptable for the 1975 season. Just how far this race has come is shown by the average speed of 62 mph turned in by the winner in conditions which, if not violent, were certainly far from the flat calm which allowed Don Aronow to set his record of 66 mph for the course in 1969.

The year 1961 was something of a fateful year for power boat racing. As well as the first Cowes/Torquay race it also saw the start of another race which has become a classic, the Viareggio to Bastia and return race; 164 miles of open water between the Italian mainland across the Ligurian sea to Corsica and back. The same year also saw the start of offshore racing for small runabouts, a class of boats which at that time were fairly lightly regarded in terms of seaworthiness. A group of British marine traders decided to prove their products by holding a one day race from Putney to Calais and return. In many ways this was quite as onerous and historic a race as those for the bigger boats. The first and last part of the race up and down the Thames took them through some of the most highly commercialised waters in the world, beset with large

72

above: Horatia has been one of the most consistant competitors in the Cowes/Torquay race and welcomes rough conditions to balance her lack of top speed compared with pure raceboats.

left: Cigarillo shows the space age approach with nothing superfluous to her purpose.

Philante at speed.

steamers, tugs, barges, and above all driftwood and other hazards to small craft. The Thames estuary is itself a difficult area for seamen in any size of vessel. After a compulsory stop at Ramsgate the little boats, sixteen to twenty feet in length, set off across the channel. Navigation is notoriously difficult at speed even in the bigger boats because of the violent motion and the difficulty of stabilising the compass. In small boats it is even worse and, fair to say, most small boat drivers were relatively unaccustomed to navigation at all. In the Cowes/Torquay race it is easy to keep England on one side to avoid getting completely lost but the Putney to Calais racers were often to be seen fanning out from Ramsgate in all directions into the open channel. The Putney/Calais became the classic for the small boats and the class itself was recognised and incorporated eventually into the range of race boats organised by the Union Internationale Motonautique, the world authority for the sport.

Class III, as it became known, started as something of the poor relation of the much grander and self important larger classes, but from humble beginnings has become the pacemaker for design, development and innovations, in Great Britain particularly. The early Levi fine-bodied racers which developed into *Surfury* and the Delta form were worked out in Class III as were the early Shead boats. The catamaran race boats started and were developed almost exclusively in Class III. The gas turbine was first applied in bigger boats but Class III are up in the hunt and a French Turbo-Meca Artouste 350-hp gas turbine weighing only 300 lb raced in 1974 together with the Wankel-engined outboards.

The small class is sub-divided into various sections to suit different power units and there is a further Class IV which caters for production boats from the assembly line and not specially designed or built for racing. Top current interest is in the OE class where support in recent years has become almost fanatical and this class in the not too distant future might become the Grand Prix type for the small raceboats.

Power boat racing is now an extremely well organised sport, very well disciplined and very well supported. It ranges from tiny inland flat water hydroplanes to marathon offshore racing for craft up to 45 feet. The principal technical problems lie in the formation of rules and regulations to keep the sport reasonably safe and within bounds and at the same time to promote excitement and development. The less a boat is in actual contact with the water the faster it will go and some aspects of the rules are devoted to stopping boats turning into low flying aeroplanes. All propulsion has, they say, to be achieved through the water and wings as such are not allowed. In order to hurry their craft along designers have re-invented a form of porpoising, once very badly thought of, to let the boat do a bit of hopping and skipping across the surface. The propeller is extended well aft and is sometimes of surface running type to keep the power push going while the hull is up and away. Another approach is the catamaran hull form. This is so well known as a standard boat shape that it is impossible to rule it out. The form offers some

above: Renato Molinari, racing in the Paris Six Hour race in 1973. His catamaran designs for circuit racing led the trend into two-hulled raceboats.

right: News of the World, a prominent raceboat of the 1960s and 1970s.

advantages of stability and in relative hull fineness, but at least part of its attraction is the fine wing form between the two hulls all ready to take advantage of the well documented aerodynamic ground effect.

In fact flying is a part of the design considerations now that boats are travelling at speeds where light aircraft take off. A bow flipped up at speed is first affected by the aerodynamic lift on the foredeck which raises it further until it stalls and the boat rapidly changes attitude and falls back more or less stern first into the sea. Modern needle-nosed boats cut this effect to the minimum and any deck lift is either broken up with deckworks or concentrated over the hull centre of gravity where it will do as much good as harm.

Speeds are getting high and development is taking an interesting parallel to the British International trophy days before the war. It is a little daunting to note that the modern boats are not yet as fast as those of forty years ago. However that may be, the risks of being thrown out of your boat increase with speed and drivers are beginning to take an interest in such fittings for themselves as parachutes. These are intended to slow down the speed at which the thrown driver actually hits the water which is quite as hard as concrete when you hit it travelling in the hundred mile an hour range.

Power boat drivers are required to have licences to prove their skill and experience. The Basic licence is more or less just bought but the National licence is only issued after an approved amount of racing experience and the International licence only comes after further racing in National events. Crash helmets have to be worn and cockpits and windscreens properly padded to reduce damage to the power boat crew. The motion in a rough race is extremely heavy and the first class raceboat driver these days has to be quite as fit as he is skilful. Although fractures do occur (and one Cowes/Torquay winner finished with a crew with a broken ankle) loss of life in the entire power boat racing sphere has been very small indeed.

Sam Griffith, who really began the whole thing, died in 1963 after a fantastic racing career during which he won every major trophy, some of them as many as four times, except for the Cowes/Torquay where he had a second prize. Among his notable achievements was the setting of a Miami to New York record in 1962 which in fact he took from that legendary figure of pre-war power boat racing, Commodore Gar Wood of the *Miss Americas*. When the World Championship series was set up for power boat racing drivers there was little argument as to who it should be named after. The Sam Griffith Memorial Trophy is awarded to the driver who sets up the maximum number of points over a series of races and currently no less than fifteen races in eight countries are eligible. The Championships were originated in 1965 when they were won by Dick Bertram and his *Moppie* boats. For the last five years they have been dominated by the Don Aronow *Cigarette* raceboats, the most successful single type in the whole history of power boat racing.

Marathon power boat racing started in 1969 with a 1,700-mile race round Britain, organised in eleven stages each intended as a successive daily event. No less than forty-two boats crossed the starting line, ranging from flat-out raceboats, through power catamarans to large, heavy, and comparatively slow, craft whose owners thought that seaworthiness might carry the day. In general, the weather was kinder than expected and fog the greater hazard. Back-up teams followed the race and quite astonishing repairs and sometimes reconstructions were achieved overnight. In due course twenty-four boats finished in accumulated course times which varied from the 39 hours of Timo Makinen in the Shead-designed *Avenger Too*, the winner, to the 85 hours taken by one of the largest craft which was last to finish.

For a while after, there was some fairly wild talk of a race clean across the Atlantic which would involve boats in fuelling rendezvous with tankers. The next big marathon, however, was ambitious enough, a race in 1971 from Westminster Pier, London, to Monte Carlo. Twenty-one boats set off on the fourteen stages and, with some bad weather to help the decimation, only six boats were officially counted as finishers. The winner was *HTS* owned by Ralph Hilton and powered with Ford diesels in an accumulated total time of 71 hours with *Zoom*, a standard Riva fast cruiser, second in 80 hours.

A 61-ft motor yacht designed by Cox & Haswell and built by Elkins.

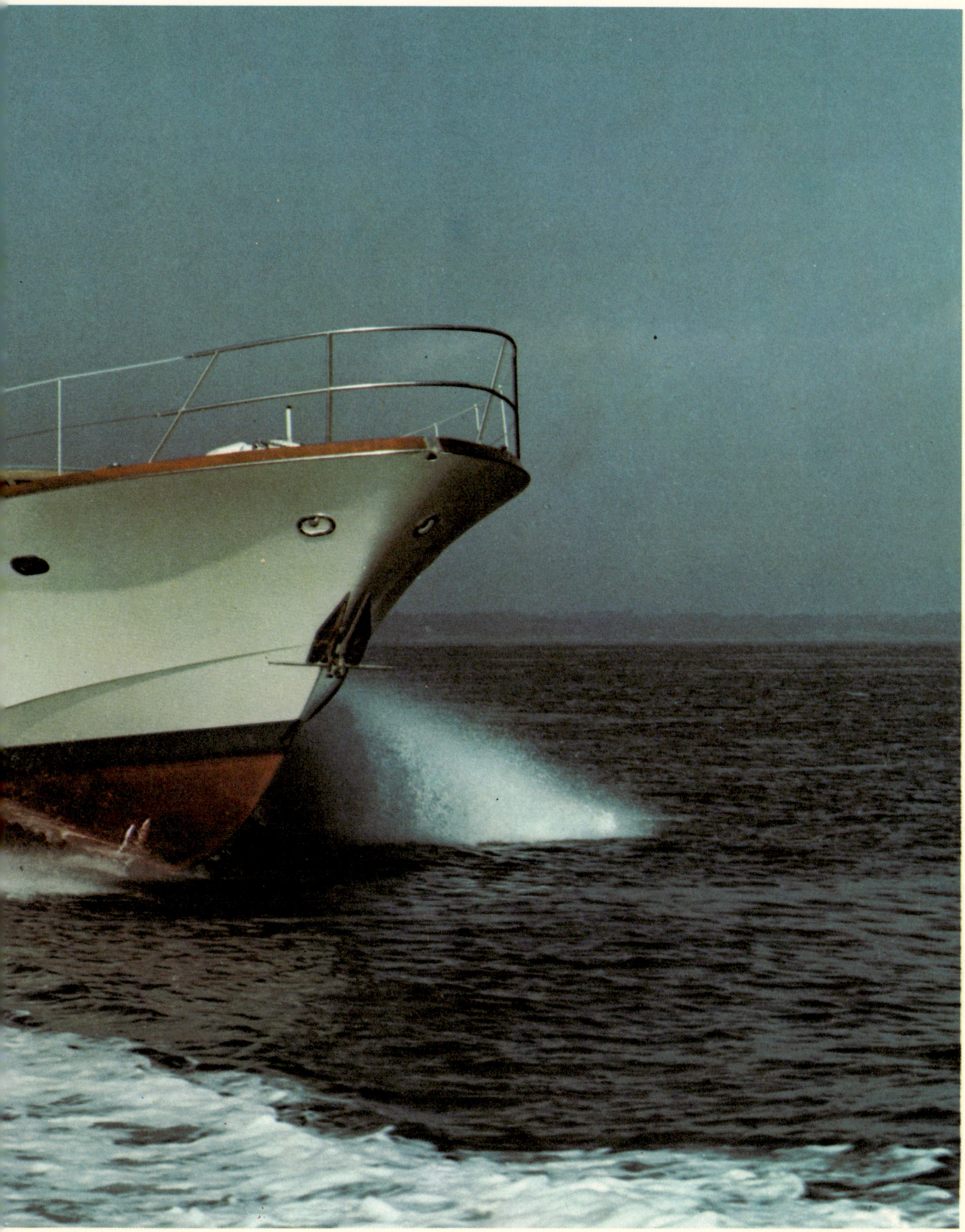

The impressive bows of *Romantica*.

Modern Yachts

A yacht is a curious possession which lies somewhere between the toy and practicality in its grossest terms. As a toy she is an extension of her owner's dreams and personality at a level well above the mundane. At the same time she is a machine to be lived in while travelling in a sometimes remarkably inhospitable environment. As a toy and personal possession she has to delight the eye, be a pleasure to operate, and in as many senses as possible, be eminently desirable. Yet again the yacht at sea is a very small closed environment containing a strictly hierarchical group who have to eat, drink, sleep and wash inside her confines while navigating her about the empty surfaces of the world and maintaining her many technical sophistications.

In the beginning of yachting craft were built by shipbuilders in the image of ships. Standards of construction and of accommodation finish were essentially exactly those of commercial ships ranging as time went on from the East Indiaman, through the clipper ships to the ocean liners. The differing wealth of yacht owners was to be seen much more in terms of size and the rareness of the woods used for panelling rather than in any marked differences in actual comfort or range of fittings.

When shipbuilding went off into iron and steel the craftsmanship of wood building was left to cater for the yachtsmen. Competition for an appreciative and generally wealthy clientele brought about a continuing rise in standards of craftsmanship until the conventional finish for a yacht from truck to keel would grace any drawing room. The craftsmanship of the wood yacht builder at its best can stand comparison with any of the best antique furniture so assiduously collected these days. And all this for use afloat among the raging deep, under the blazing sun, and in a generally corrosive atmosphere.

The particular craftsmanship in wood is disappearing with wood itself but extremely high standards of finish and fittings are still considered the conventional norm for modern yachts. The Italian Cantieri Riva company are acknowledged leaders and standard setters for beautiful finishes. Traditionally they are known for a range of open speed boats and runabouts of conservative hull form. These are of a varnished wood finish although the word varnish seems out of place compared with the actual super polish gloss which they achieve. Riva have recently extended their craftsmanship into bigger cabin boats with American deep vee hulls, and to demonstrate how their workmanship extends well beyond the surface finish won second prize in the London/Monte Carlo marathon power boat race.

The old-fashioned conventionally planked wood hulls, beautifully built and brimming with craft skill as they were, have, thankfully, more or less disappeared. Their intricate and interwoven structures involving a thousand different parts were only acceptable when there was nothing better, and now there is. Principal among the new materials is, of course, glass reinforced plastics (grp) forming one piece moulded hulls capable of logical structuring and complete watertightness. Mould costs are high and such a construction is only financially attractive when there are several craft to be built. Inevitably it was first introduced at the small end of the market where numbers are high but now it has crept up to quite sizable craft. At this moment the Halmatic company has possibly the largest mould for motor yacht hulls to a design by Hargrave. The first yacht out of the mould was *Mariola* finished by Camper & Nicholsons and when launched she was the largest private grp yacht afloat anywhere. For production boats up to, say, 50 feet in length grp currently has a good edge on all other forms of construction.

Above fifty feet the one-off type of yacht gets more and more usual as size increases. A great many, probably most, are of metal construction either of welded steel or welded aluminium. The rivetted construction hulls were fine in the larger sizes where they had ship-type maintenance and where indeed their longevity was only compared with ships. In small sizes, however, possibly aided by neglect when the yacht was out of commission in the winter months, steel hulls had something of a poor reputation for rusting. After a time this required expensive replating but in the meantime also tended to show ugly rust streaks inside and out. Condensation on the metal was itself both unattractive to live with and a further cause of rusting. The welded hull improves the picture somewhat with

81

right: The saloon of the 55-foot Souter-built *Chardon*.

below right: The main saloon of *Lucy III*.
below: The engine-room of *Lucy III*.

82

almost complete freedom from ledges and crannies where water lingers and the rust starts. Many of the better quality hulls are sand blasted clean and zinc sprayed and nowadays plastics coatings on the metal can give a great deal of protection. The modern steel hull, well built and finished, is a far cry from some of the cheaply built rust buckets which are to be seen mouldering away as houseboats. Condensation is also largely catered for by foam plastics insulation bonded directly to the interior faces of the metal, reducing at the same time noise and heat.

There was a time when aluminium hulls had something of a bad name owing to the somewhat perilous position of the metal in the galvanic table. With rivetted construction a destructive current could be set up between the different constituents of the plates and rivets leading to a deterioration of the latter. The introduction of the new welding alloys a few years ago and the enormously improved electrical installation of recent times have changed the picture and aluminium construction is now both practical and fashionable. Uffa Fox once expressed the immortal opinion that only an idiot would carry a steam roller with him when putting to sea. The power/weight ratio is paramount in boat performance as in most things and aluminium construction is up to a third lighter than, say, steel or grp. It is an expensive material but over the life of the yacht the extra expense may well be returned in reduced maintenance costs and lighter fuel bills for the same running speeds. Aluminium also has the pleasant

above: The Shead-designed *Enfield Avenger* under construction in aluminium at Enfield Marine.

right: The basic bones of a 62-foot motor yacht building at Bideford.

characteristic for yachts of good thermal conductivity which allows the direct heat of a baking sun to be run off, so to speak, more quickly than does, say, steel or grp. This keeps an aluminium hull somewhat cooler in a hot climate. It is also a pleasant material to live with, almost as pleasant as wood. Aluminium deckworks are often to be seen on steel or even wooden vessels. Mostly this is both to save weight and to reduce top weight but the possibilities of easier panel rolling and panel beating also allow the economic development of handsome shapes to suit the styling.

Wood, as a material for building yachts, is far from dead. When used in an all-glued construction it can form a homogeneous skin and structure lighter than steel or grp and comparable to aluminium. In fact as a generally lively material the glued or laminated wood constructions are highly suitable for performance craft. In particular the so-called moulded plywood constructions show the benefits of wood off to the best advantage. The skin of the craft is laminated from layer after layer of wood veneers until it forms a monocoque structure in its own right to which a minimum of additional structure has to be added. With such a multi-skin approach the various parts and layers can be of different materials and to some extent the skin itself can therefore be engineered to the required characteristics much as in a grp hull. Wood is both light and springy and the finished moulded wood boat hull often shows advantages in performance. It is not however a cheap construction and only the most limited amount of production technique can be applied. An elaborate mould has to be made to build the skin on and each veneer plank is hand fitted into place.

Two yards which have made a big name for using moulded construction are W. A. Souter and Son of Cowes who specialise in a cold setting process and Fairey Marine of Hamble, who as heirs to wartime autoclave equipment used for producing wooden aircraft, use a hot setting glue system. Souters have built moulded craft up to eighty feet in length while Faireys specialize in semi-production craft of much smaller dimensions.

A great many wooden yachts of considerable size are built in a more conventional form with a bodywork of frames and keel clad directly in two or more layers of relatively thick planking run diagonally in different directions in each layer. For the sake of appearance the outside layer is often run fore and aft exactly as traditional carvel construction so that the finished hull of the yacht looks little changed from the past. The use of marine glue throughout has however bonded her into a relatively watertight whole without need for caulking.

It is surprising how often the decks, in a yacht of any type of construction, are built with laid teak planking. Teak is a beautiful wood but, for scrubbed decking, extremely vulnerable to sun tan oil and cigarettes. The planks have to be quite narrow, as little as two inches perhaps, to reduce swelling and shrinking movement between a soaking at sea with salt water and a dry month in harbour open to hot sun. The gaps between the planks are filled with a rubber compound to cater for the minor movements that do occur and the whole forms an extremely elaborate and somewhat vulnerable walking surface. In the old days the seaming compounds also had to stop water dripping directly through into the accommodation. Nowadays the teak decks are usually fitted over a complete under deck, usually of plywood. The only excuses for continued use are first, the pleasant shippiness they give to the vessel, and secondly, that there can be little doubt that laid teak decks are still the best non-slip finish you can fit and live with. The non-slip patterned decking materials and the sanded paint approaches are quite efficient when seafaring but terrible to sun bathe on.

right: The main saloon of *Stilvi*, looking forward.
below: A guest cabin on board the yacht *Stilvi*.

left: The Tiger C42 sportsboat *Ronny Boy* designed by Paolo Caliari as both a yacht and a raceboat.

below: A view of the cabin of *Ronny Boy.*

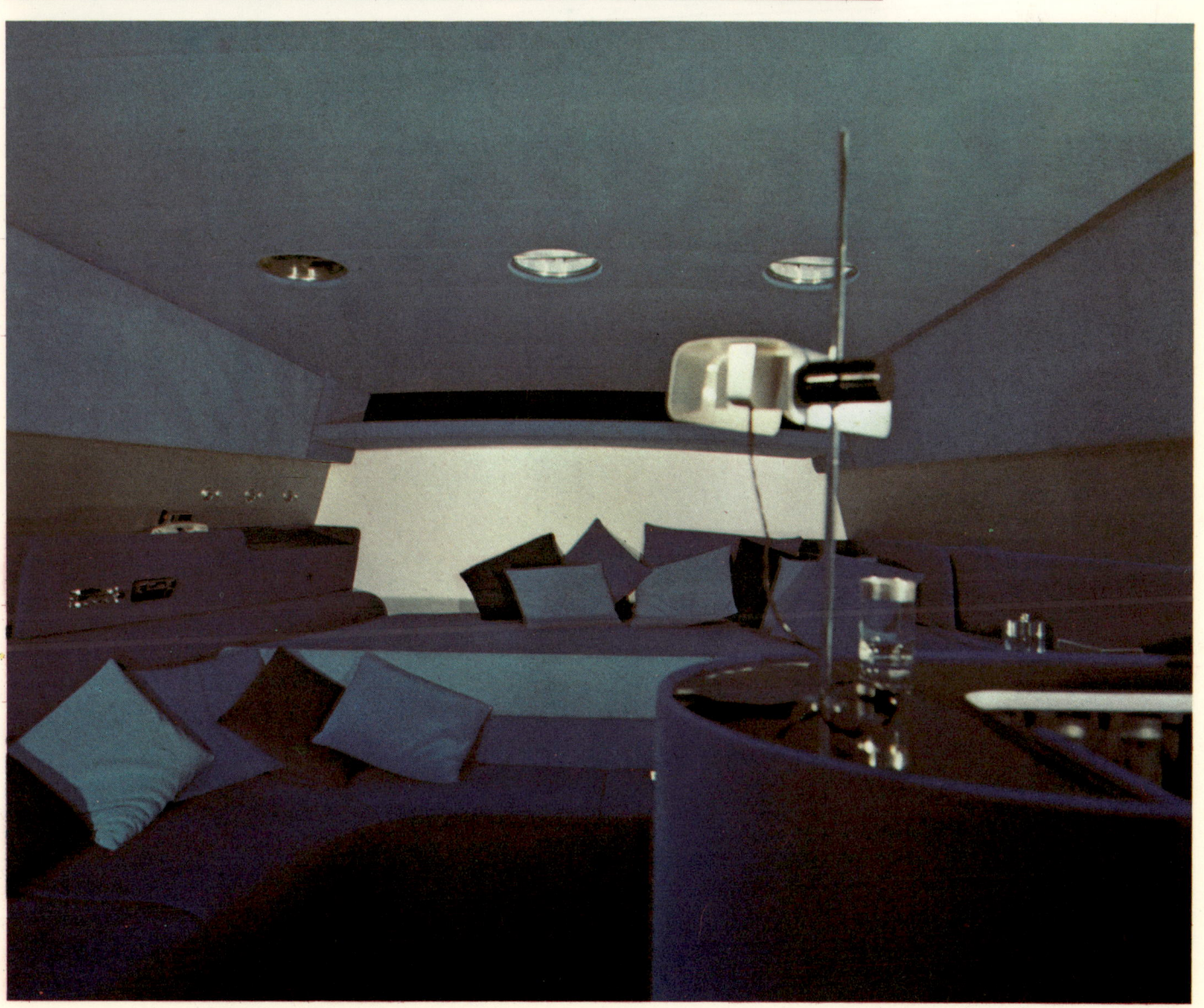

Concrete construction is still gaining ground among pleasure boats. It is unfortunately named perhaps for it really refers to a quite sophisticated reinforced homogeneous skin construction. It has a basic virtue, widely quoted, of being a cheap construction. However, halving the costs of the hull in fact will reduce the overall cost of a yacht by only about one sixth while digging in quite deeply into its resale value. The construction also relies heavily on an initial structure which cannot be inspected after plastering and the whole probity of the hull depends extensively on the skill used both in the plastering and in the two weeks or so taken in drying it out. The beautiful finish necessary for a yacht to be a yacht has then to be applied to the hull, another area of highly skilled work.

Big yachts are generally fairly conservative in hull design and performance partly from the owner's complete lack of any desire to push the frontiers of naval architecture along with his spending money and partly because, very often, his or her standards were set a few years earlier, before the cash became available. There is in any case a generally accepted speed at any one time which is considered proper for a yacht. After the war it was of the order of ten knots, a few years ago it rose to twelve and then fifteen and now it is twenty. This is craft speed independent of size which means that the bigger yachts are generally operating in a relatively lower speed band compared with smaller craft. Today's yacht is assessed much more on its size and opulence rather than in terms of seaworthiness, manoeuvrability, or even the exact details of speed. All these basic requirements in the present state of the yacht designer's art are confidently expected to be satisfactory, and the invidious comparisons, boat for boat, are really made in other departments.

In smaller craft the advent of the new constructions has allowed a fairly adventurous approach to be made to hull form including several possibilities which would have been practically impossible in planked wood. Perhaps the most striking of the recent fashions has been the re-emergence of the power multi-hull vessel. In the most early days of power afloat the catamaran and even the trimaran was quite often used as a convenient stable base for carrying the weight and height of the mechanical systems. The multi-hull came into fashion again for sailing boats soon after the war. Henry Kaiser built a large catamaran power yacht which was, as they say, 'successful 'til it sank', the catamaran type being extremely vulnerable to damage. The stresses built up in its gantry form in a seaway can be high and a leak in one hull requires special watertight measures if she is to remain reasonably safely afloat. The advantages of the catamaran form lie principally with sailing craft but for power boats they offer a wide platform of greatly reduced rolling characteristics on which to build accommodation. The disadvantages lie in the increased costs of building more than one hull for your yacht and the separation of essential parts of her systems. There is some feeling that the long fine hulls will give her more speed for the same horsepower. This may be true in some parts of the total speed range but for normal pleasure yacht speeds this has yet to be proved. The trimaran is in essence something of a compromise between the advantages of the single hull for accommodation and easy motion and the stability and deck area of the catamaran. Unfortunately the costs of three hulls must be more than for two or one and this cost cannot, in a power yacht, be set against the cost of a lead keel as for a sailing vessel. The multi-hull yacht is therefore normally built only for an owner with some specialised interest. It is, for instance, an extremely stable platform for underwater archaeology diving, an excellent deck area for some forms of open water fishing and scarcely beatable for flat water bathing parties.

The compromise forms are more usually seen in the very small craft, particularly those of a somewhat rectangular deck plan. The hull is moulded into a rather complex shape which may vary from a single tunnel form to a fairly normal vee plus additional planing surfaces spread right out to the maximum beam to give stability. Such forms are often excellent in moderate seas but with a distinct limit on speed in really rough water compared with, for instance, the long thin fine hull forms developed for racing boats. The criteria for the modern yacht is principally, almost overwhelmingly, one of appearance. A yacht of perfect beauty will be forgiven all manner of shortcomings in other departments while the converse, the ugly yacht, will never be forgiven for anything at all. Nowadays a yacht spends a great deal of her time moored stern to onto the quay in harbour. Her external appearance has therefore to be appreciated in three separate directions. First when other yachts are coming into harbour all that will be seen of her is a bow among a row of bows. The modern yacht therefore tends to have an extremely fine looking bow, often with a heavy and distinctive rake. Second, guests and the rest of the world will mainly see her stern with its gangway to the quay among a row of similar gangways. The stern is the 'front door' of the yacht and must be striking in its own right with a handsome deckhouse end, usually with multiple opening doors to the saloon. The third criteria is that she be photogenic. For a considerable proportion of each year her owner may well be working himself silly to be able to afford her and all he will have to remind himself of his beautiful yacht will be the pile of bills and a collection of photographs.

Marinas or specialised yacht harbours are growing everywhere there is yachting and are extremely popular with power yachts as well as sail. The convenience of a secure individual berth with electricity, water and telephones all laid on, plus somewhere to park the car, is almost overwhelming for carefree life in harbour. Charges are usually on the basis of length and there was a period when this had something of a heavy hand on yacht design with accommodation being packed into the shortest possible hull. Fortunately this seems to have changed and yachts are getting bigger again in sheer physical dimensions. The extra cost of a complex installation which has to be packed in and around an over-full accommodation plan is showing up in increased labour costs both for the installation and in

The owner's stateroom of the Vosper-built *Romantica*.

its maintenance. Now it is recognised that the hull is only a modest part of the cost of a yacht and that it is economical to make her bigger if the extra space is devoted to simplifying the installations. Some yachts are fitted with proper systems tunnels where a high degree of maintenance and repairs can be achieved without disturbing the owner and his guests. Indeed it is reported that in one yacht it was possible to clear a blocked bath drain with the owner's wife *in situ* and unaware that there was any kind of problem.

In the old days the machinery and anything of that order of technology was tolerated rather than appreciated by the owner and his guests. In fact all the smellier aspects of life afloat, the engines, the galley, and so on, were often lumped right up forward with the crew in their forecastle. The prevailing draught inside a boat on moorings or under way is a counter current which blows from aft to forward. Smells therefore rarely percolated back to the saloon to discommode the gentry. Engines in particular were only just tolerated and few owners really wanted to get their hands dirty and their white flannels covered in black grease from too close an interest. Now there is a trend in the opposite direction as technology itself becomes fashionable. Engines and engine rooms are laid out and

above: The modern profile of the Tarquin 65.

right: When launched by Camper & Nicholsons in 1972 *Mariola*, at 85 feet, was the largest private grp yacht afloat.

constructed essentially to be clean and the guests increasingly invited to see the beautiful and expensive propulsion and auxiliary machinery. It is becoming common to fit a separate control room with double glazed windows into the engine room. Here, the engineer, and more important the guests, can take an interest in the machinery without the excesses of noise and heat which often occur in a high speed engine room. One yacht is even planned with engine room 'Son et Lumiere' and a running commentary in several languages. The appropriate tape is popped into the slot and spotlights and coloured lights illuminate the various parts of the machinery as they are explained through the control room speakers. Apart from amusing his guests this close interest in the machinery also ensures the owner an equally devoted interest in it by his crew.

Another slightly unusual amusement developing in the modern yacht is navigation itself. At one level this is of serious interest to the professional captain who has to navigate the yacht and its precious burdens safely. At another the current pleasure which quite untechnical people take in the wonderful world of electronics spills over into an avid interest in such things as the radar scan and the depth of water, wind speed and direction, and even the co-ordinate position of the yacht as given in figures on the navigation machine. To cater for this interest the navigation instruments have to be redesigned and displayed so that they can be seen by a number of people at any time. The radar scan, for instance, can be

above: In a yacht of any size it is possible to furnish the main cabins with normal household furniture. This shows the saloon of *Romantica*.

right: The owner's stateroom of the Grand Banks 48 built by American Marine in Hong Kong, showing the extensive use of custom-made furniture.

shown on a big screen either by projection or by a closed circuit television arrangement. In the same vein electronic calculators and the minor computers are for many people a great deal of pleasure to use. Navigation problems can be solved by a magnetic or punched card programme popped into the bridge computer by any unskilled hand which can then go on to punch in the figures and receive an accurate answer.

Television is as much a standard fitting to the yacht afloat as it is to the house ashore. Even closed circuit television is a comparatively small additional cost compared with the whole vessel and a large yacht may well have an underwater TV camera for looking at passing dolphins and the exotic tropical seabeds in clear water. A second camera might also be fitted to the bridge top where it can be trained on passing points of interest. This sounds blasé and effete in the extreme but it is true that on board a yacht there are so many things to look at that it is quite restful to be fitted with the additional watchful eye. All the more normal household electronics are also commonly fitted, such as multi-channel sound, domestic radio, tape recorders, and so on. In fact the yacht, as a holiday home and very personal possession, is quite often much better equipped with such good things than the house of the owner.

Yachting used to be identified with the healthy life of heaving on tarry ropes and salt water showers. Fortunately, or unfortunately, depending on your point of view, this is no longer so. The exercise and so on is now no more automatic afloat than it is ashore. Quite small yachts, for instance, can be fitted with lifts to prevent the labour of climbing companion staircases and even the mechanical crow's nest is in sight. Instead of climbing the mast to the look-out position this will now power down to deck level and back at the touch of the appropriate buttons so that even the most unfit can enjoy the view. There was once some exercise in shore excursions and in walking to and fro in the yacht harbour. Now it is common to carry midget motor bikes on board, not uncommon to find a small car, with garage, on board, and the helicopter is no longer a status symbol of any rarity. Many larger yachts are now built with an area of deck designated and specially strengthened for the helicopter landing pad.

Power anchor winches have been common since the days of steam but hydraulic cranes are increasingly being used for handling boats and stores. There is practically nowhere for the yachtsman to get exercise unless he sets his mind to it. In fact the sauna is a common fitting and the small gymnasium is following it. Under water swimming is another obvious associated sport and many large motor yachts will carry compressors for refilling air bottles. Then there is water ski-ing, also, of course associated with yachting, and most yachts of almost any size carry a tender which can go fast enough to pull a water skier up. Many, especially the smaller craft, use rubber boats, a post-war growth on the yachting scene. They are generally far from pretty and look quite odd hanging from the davits of some enamelled gem of the yacht builders' art. Few however could impugn their usefulness and practicability as a yacht tender. They are soft and scratch free when alongside the yacht, light to pull up the hard or the beach and safe for quite inexperienced drivers to run at speed. Further, they can be deflated and stored out of the sun when not required, double up as life rafts in that kind of disaster, and have the most useful characteristics of acting as giant fenders should the yacht be forced by wind and waves to lie against, say, jagged pier pilings. Bigger yachts tend to have a rubber boat but carry as well a small speed boat or runabout, plus possibly a sailing dinghy. The biggest craft might well carry a Riva runabout thereby practically starting the yachting cycle once again.

Oddly enough the latest feature to be fitted on board yachts of any size is a swimming pool. Partly due to the yachts themselves a great many harbours are filthy with pollution and it is said that indeed large areas of the Mediterranean sea are becoming suspect for safety. The harbour authorities are, one by one, bringing in new and restrictive laws about the discharge of waste from yachts but for many years the damage has been done. Since swimming is at its best for pleasure in sea surroundings what more can the poor yacht owner do than swim in his own pool a few feet clear above the sea.

below: The Riva *Summertime* with two 200-hp diesels and a modern deep Vee hull. Note the Mediterranean gangway left mounted aft under way.

bottom: The 235-foot *La Belle Simone*, designed by Rinaldo Gastaldi.

below: The Riva *Superamerica,* a modern 42-ft yacht.

Index

Figures in italics refer to illustrations

Admiral Popov 22
Aeromarine IX 72
Aetea 37
Aitken, Sir Max 61
Alagi 14
Alberta 23
Alexander, Czar 22
Allison engines 18
Amazone 26
America 37–8
America's Cup 27
Apel, Arno 16
Aronow, Don 69, 72, 77
A'Speranziella 64, *64*, 65
Assheton Smith, T. 21
Astilleros Udondo 32
Avenger Too *67*, 77
Avila 32

Baglietto 36
Bain, John 31
Baltic Sea 31
Benetti 37
Bennett, James Gordon 22
Bertram, Dick *64*, 65, 77
Beryl jet engines 19
Biscay, Bay of 32
Black Maria 68
Black Panther 46
Black Tornado 72
Bluebird *12*, 16; three-pointer *14*, 16, *17*; jet propulsion 18; prop-rider 19; Orpheus jet engine *18*, 19
Blue Moppie *64*, 65
Bonelli, Ronnie 72
Brassey, Lord 21
Brave Moppie 65
Bristol Proteus engines 37
British International Trophy 61; *see also* Harmsworth Trophy
British Power Boat Company

Cadiz 32
Camanda *33*, 36, 37
Camper and Nicholsons 26, 27, 37
Campbell, Donald 18–9
Campbell, Sir Malcolm 15, 16, 18
Cantieri Riva 81
Carol of Rumania, King 26
Casson, Sir Hugh 36
Catamarans 75, *76*
Caterpillar engines 38
Chardon 82
Chris Craft 37
Cigarette 69
Cigarette-type race boats *71*, 72, 77
Cigarillo 73
Circular yachts 22, *23*
Classes: ON *51*; OP type 68; III 75; IV 75; SE 75; OE 75
Clermont 7
Clyde, River 21
Coastal motor boats 15, 16
Cobb, John 19
Coniston, Lake 18
Copper, Fred 15, 16
Cowes 21, 36, 68
Cowes/Torquay race 61, 65, 68, 69–72
Cox and Haswell 37, *78*
Crest Cutter 36, 37
Crise, Red 61
Cross-Channel race (1904) 9
Crusader *17*, 19, 44
Cummins engines 32, 36, 37
Cutty Sark 26, 27

Daimler, Gottlieb 9
Daimler engines *41*
Daytona engines *56*, 65, 68, 69
De Havilland engines; Ghost 44; Goblin jet *17*, 18, 19
Delta Synthesis 68
Denny 22
Deutz engines 32

Diesel yachts 26, 27
Dixie 10
Dixie II 10
Dixie III 13
Don, Kaye 15
Dry Martini 72
Du Cane, Peter 16, 19

Edge, S. F. 9
Elder, John 22
Elettra see Rovensha
Elfin 20, 21
Enfield Avenger 70, 84
Engine design 41–57

Fairey Marine 85
Fairy 21
Fitch, John 7
Ford Sabre engines *49*
Fox, Uffa *68*, 83

Garden, William 38
Gardner, Charles 65
Gardner, Jimmy 65
Gardner engines 37
Gas turbine boats 72, 75
Gay Bombardier 18
General Motors engines 32
Ghostrider *60*, 68
Giles, Laurent 29, 31, 37
Gipsy Girl 68
Glass Moppie 64
Glencairn see Liberty
Gleniffer engines 29
Gold Cup 15
Grand Banks 48 *52*, 92
Griffith, Sam 61, 64, *64*, 65, 77
Grocco-Ricaldone hydrofoil *8*
Gulf Stream 37
Gulzar 26

Halmatic Company 81
Harmsworth, Sir Alfred (Lord Northcliffe) 9
Harmsworth Trophy 9, 10, 13, 15
Hatteras *36*, 38
Hedonist *34*, 37
Herreshoff, Nathaniel 8, 9
Hildur 38
Hilton, Ralph 77
Horatio 73
HTS 72, 77
Houston, Dame Lucy 24
Houston, Sir Robert 24
Hulls, Jonathon 7
Hunt, Raymond 36, 65
Hydrofoils: Grocco-Ricaldone *8*
Hydroplanes *8*, 13, 15, *43*
Hydrosonic Special 55

Internal combustion engine 9
Isle III 32
Isotta Fraschini engines 65

Jackie S 65
Jester 29
John Brown, Clydebank 26

Kaiser, Henry 88
Kaiseradler 23
Kakki M 38
Kelvin engines *48*
Keswick, Major 26
Kiekhaefer Aeromarine engines 72

La Belle Simone 94
Lady Nara 72
Laura 3a 19
Lenoir, J. J. E. 9
Levi, Renato 64, 65
Liberty (Glencairn) 24, *25*
Little Juliana 7
Livadia 22
London/Monte Carlo race 77, 81
Long Island Sound 21
Luceafarul 26

Lucky Moppie 65
Lucy III 82
Lurssen, Fr 29
Lyme Bay 64, 68, 69
Lysistrata 22

Maggiore, Lake 16
Makinen, Timo 77
MAN engines 27
Maple Leaf IV *8*, 13, 15
Marconi, Guglielmo 24
Mariola 81, *90*
Maureen Mhor 28
Meche III 32
Mediterranean Sea 32
Menai 21
Mercedes IV 9
Mercury 30, 37, *52*
Mercury engines *56*
Miller, Patrick 7
Miranda III 15
Miranda IV 15
Miss America 10, 15
Miss America II 15
Miss America VII 15
Miss America VIII 15
Miss America IX 15
Miss America X 15, *49*
Miss Britain III 12, 15
Miss Embassy 72
Miss Enfield 69
Miss Enfield II 69
Miss England II 10, 15, 44
Miss England III 10, 15
Miss Guernsey 47
Miss Supertest III 61
Molinari, Renato 76
Motor boats
Motor yachts 26–7, *78, 84*

Nahlin *25*, 26
Napier I 9
Napier engines 9; Lion 15
Napier Minor 9
New Orleans engines 13
News of the World 76
Niarchos, Stravros 37
Nicopao 72
Norge 27, *28*
North Sea 31

Orpheus jet engines 19
Osborne 21
Otto, Dr 9

Packard engines 16, *49*
Paddle steamers 7
Paddle yachts 21, 23
Panhard engines 9
Paris Six Hour race *43*, *50*
Parsons, Sir Charles 9
Parsons engines *41*
Pearson, Hon. Michael 37
Petroni, Commander 72
Philante 27, *28*, 74
Piet Hein 29
Pioneer 13
Planing 10–13
Popov, Admiral 22
Porpoising 13
Priestman internal combustion engine 9
Prop riding 19
Putney/Calais race 72, 75

Queenstown (Cobh) 9

Radar 57
Ramage and Ferguson 22
Ramus, Rev. 13
Red Tornado 59
Richey, Michael 65
Rolls-Royce engines 15, 16, 72
Romantica *34*, *80*, *89*, *92*
Ronny Boy 87

Rovensha (Elettra) 22, 27
Rover engines 37
Royal Air Force Sea Rescue 64
Royal Motor Yacht Club 61, 64
Royal Navy 64
Royal Northern Yacht Club 21
Royal Torbay Yacht Club 64
Royal Yacht Squadron 21, 64

Sam Griffith Memorial Trophy 77
Saunders Roe 15, 16
Savundra, Dr 65
Sayers, Stanley 18, 19
Scott-Paine, Hubert 15, 16
Segrave, Sir Henry 15
Shandau 31
Shead, Don 69, 72
Shorter, Edward 7
Silver, James 29
Slo-Mo-Shun IV *17*, 18–19
Sopwith, T. O. M. 27, 64, 68, 72
Souter and Son, W. A. 36, 68, 85
Spirit of Ecstacy 68
Steam turbines 9, 26
Steam yachts 21–6, *25*, 27
Stevens, Colonel John 7
Stilvi 86
Stork engines 29
Straight, Whitney 36
Summertime 94
Sunbeam 21
Superamerica 95
Super Aquarama 55
Surfrider 65
Surfury *62*, 65, 68, 75
Swiftsure 9

Tadorna 26
Tagus, River 32
Tamahine *28*, 29
Tarquin 65, 90
Telstar 68, 69
Thornycroft, Sir John 13, 15
Thornycrofts 26
Thorneywork, Peter *51*
Thunderbolt 64
Thunderfish 55
Together IV 32
Torpedo boats 15
Tramontana II *63*, 65
Tredegar, Lord 24
Trenora 26
Tubo-Meca Artouste 75
Turbinia *8*, 9, 41
Twin screw 7

Union International Motonautique 75
Unowot 38, 72
Ursula 10

Valvanera III 32
Van Lent and Zonen, C. 32
Verga, Mario 19
Viareggio/Bastia race 72
Victoria and Albert 21
Vingt-et-Un II 9
Vospers 16, 29, 37, 65, 72
Vries Lentsch, de 32

Wakefield, Lord 15
Watson, G. L. 22
Wave making 8
Westlake III 32
Westminster, Duke of 10, 13, 26
Wilkins, Dick 65
Windemere, Lake 15
Wishnick, Bill 72
Wood, Commodore Garfield 15, *49*, 77
Woodpecker 31, *33*
World Championship 77
Wynne, Jim 64, 68

Yarrow 26
Yo-Yo 64
Yule, Lady 26

Zoom *66*, 77

Acknowledgments

The publishers gratefully acknowledge the following sources for providing the illustrations indicated:

Colour: Beken of Cowes Ltd front cover; Colour Library International Ltd 42/43 bottom, 62/63, 71; Sergio Gramaglia 87 top and bottom; Hamlyn Group Picture Library 34 top; E. D. Lacey 58, 58/59; London Express News and Feature Services 54/55, 55, 63 inset, 67 inset; Brian Manby 78/79, 82–83, 86 top and bottom, 90–91; Picturepoint Ltd 34/35, 35 top, 38/39, 42/43 top, 46–47, 50, 62 inset, 66/67, 70, 74/75; Rapho 94 bottom; John Watney 54, 94 top, 95 and back cover.

Black and white: American Marine Ltd 52 top, 93; Barnabys Picture Library 57; Beken of Cowes Ltd front endpaper, title page, 9 top, 10 top, 11 top, 20/21, 23 centre and bottom, 24–25, 28 top, 29–33, 64, 69, 80; Cantieri Baglietto S.p.A. 8 bottom, 14 top; Central Press Photos Ltd 12/13 bottom, 44 top; Science Museum, London (Crown Copyright) 6/7, 40/41, 41; Enfield Marine Ltd 84; Esso contents page, 60/61; Ford 49 bottom, back endpaper; Fox Photos Ltd 11 bottom, 17, 44 centre; GEC Diesels Ltd 48; Hamlyn Group Picture Library 16 bottom; Hatteras Yachts 36 bottom; JBS Associates Ltd 56 left; Motor Boat and Yachting 36 top, 49 top, 65, 68/69, 72/73, 76; The National Maritime Museum, London 8 top, 9 bottom, 12/13 top, 23 top; Ocean Publications Ltd 76/77; Popperfoto 10 bottom, 16 top, 18, 19; Radio Times Hulton Picture Library 26, 27; T.T. Boat Designs Ltd 73; Vosper Thornycroft Ltd 14 bottom, 44 bottom, 52 bottom, 89, 92; G. L. Watson & Co. Ltd 28 bottom.

The following illustrations are reproduced by kind permission of: Aquarius Yacht Co. 90/91 top; Camper & Nicholson 82, 83, 86 top and bottom, 90/91 bottom; Caterpillar Tractor Co. Ltd 73; Daily Express 76/77; E. F. Elkins Ltd 78/79; Royal Geographical Society, London 34 top; Philip T. Smith 36 top.